The old farmer's almanac for kids
J 031.02
D0981102
Silver City

YANKEE PUBLISHING
INCORPORATED

SILVER CITY PUBLIC LIBRARY
515 W. COLLEGE AVE.
SILVER CITY, NM 88061

J
031.02
Old

10.00

252986

1/12

Text, design, and compilation © 2011 by Yankee Publishing Inc. All rights reserved. No part of this publication may be reproduced or transmitted in any form or by any means, electronic or mechanical, including photocopy, recording, or any other information storage and retrieval system, without the written permission of the publisher.

***The Old Farmer's Almanac* Books**

Publisher: Sherin Pierce

Series editor: Janice Stillman
Art director: Margo Letourneau
Copy editor: Jack Burnett
Contributors: Bob Berman, Aldo P. Biagiotti, Jack Burnett, Alice Cary, Gregory Danner, Mare-Anne Jarvela, Martie Majoros, Amy Nieskens, Sarah Perreault, Sara Schultz, Luisa Silveri, Heidi Stonehill

V.P., New Media and Production: Paul Belliveau
Production directors: Susan Gross, David Ziarnowski
Production artists: Lucille Rines, Rachel Kipka, Janet Grant

Companion Web site: Almanac4kids.com
Web editor: Catherine Boeckmann; **Web designer:** Lou S. Eastman
Web design associate: Amy Bidder; **E-commerce manager:** Alan Henning
Programming: Reinvented, Inc.

For additional information about this and other publications from *The Old Farmer's Almanac,* visit **Almanac.com** or call **1-800-ALMANAC**

Distributed in the book trade in the United States by Houghton Mifflin Harcourt and in Canada by Thomas Allen & Son Limited

Direct-to-retail and bulk sales are handled by Cindy Schlosser, 800-729-9265, ext. 126, or Stacey Korpi, ext. 160

Yankee Publishing Inc., P.O. Box 520,
1121 Main Street, Dublin, New Hampshire 03444

ISBN-13: 978-1-57198-554-5
ISSN: 1948-061X

FIRST PRINTING OF VOLUME 4

Thank you to everyone who had a hand in producing this Almanac and getting it to market, including printers, distributors, and sales and delivery people.

PRINTED IN THE UNITED STATES OF AMERICA

Hey, Kids!

Here we—and you—go again! This edition of **The Old Farmer's Almanac for Kids** has more facts, more fun, more activities, more stories, more of **everything** because you and other kids told us that you wanted **more.**

We hope that you have hours of fun reading this book, sharing it with your family and friends, trying the activities, telling the riddles, playing the games—and then doing it all over again.

Be sure to visit this book's Web site, **Almanac4kids.com.** You'll find even more of everything there. While you're at it, use "Tell Us" to let us know what you think of the site and how you like this Almanac.

Finally, be sure to thank the person who bought this book and gave it to you. Then, thank him or her for us, too.

Now, turn the page and **have fun!**

The Editors

P.S. You can help us make Volume 5 even more fun and fascinating by participating in our quick and easy questionnaire: Go to **Almanac.com/Kids4Survey.** Thanks!

Calendar

Astronomy

Weather

79

Nature

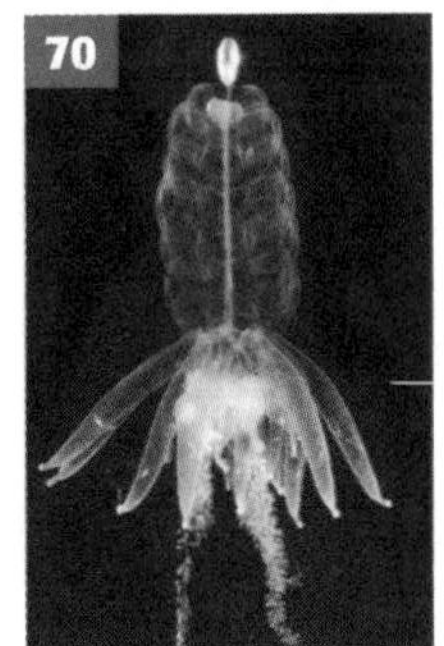

In the Garden

On the Farm

(continued on next page) ➡

CONTENTS (continued)

Pets

Sports

Crafts

Health

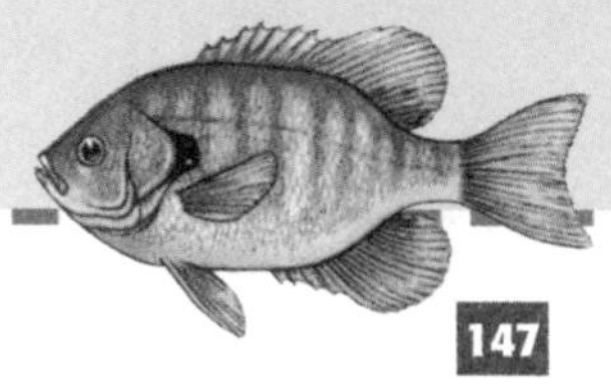

147

Amusement

179

160

THE 13TH

HOW LUCKY IS IT?

Wrap Your Tongue Around This ➡ Triskaidekaphobia.

(Sound it out: **triss-kye-deck-uh-FO-be-uh.**) That's the word for the fear of the number 13. If you've got it, you're not alone. But really: **Are 13s unlucky?** You decide:

- In years past, ocean liners scheduled to leave port on the **13th** (Friday or not) would often delay their departures until after midnight. Even now, some people simply won't travel on that day.

- A "baker's dozen" is **13** (not 12).

- There were **13** original colonies in what would become the United States.

- The Great Seal of the United States contains **13** stars, **13** stripes, and an eagle, with **13** tail feathers, that holds **13** arrows and an olive branch with **13** leaves.
- The U.S. motto, *"E Pluribus Unum,"* which means "out of many, one," has **13** letters.

FUTURE FRIDAYS

These days are all **Fridays the 13th**:

2012: January 13, April 13, July 13
2013: September 13, December 13
2014: June 13
2015: February 13, March 13, November 13
2016: May 13
2017: January 13, October 13
2018: April 13, July 13
2019: September 13, December 13
2020: March 13, November 13

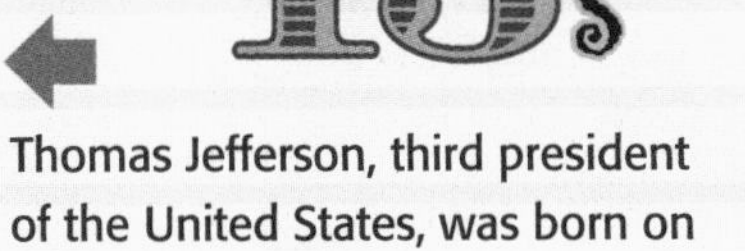

HISTORIC 13s

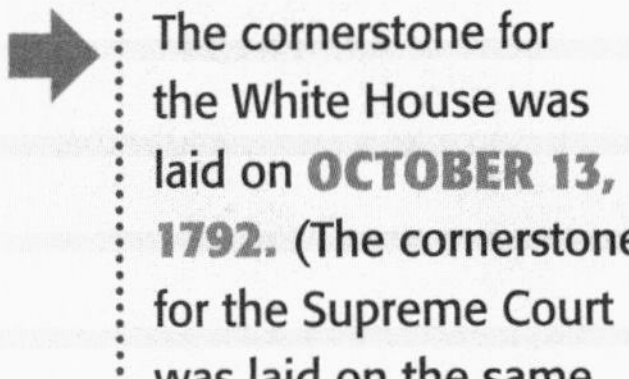

Thomas Jefferson, third president of the United States, was born on **APRIL 13, 1743.**

Horatio Alger, author of boys' adventure stories, was born on **JANUARY 13, 1834.**

The cornerstone for the White House was laid on **OCTOBER 13, 1792.** (The cornerstone for the Supreme Court was laid on the same date in 1932.)

continued ···

On **SEPTEMBER 13, 1857,** Milton S. Hershey, candy-maker, was born. He died on **OCTOBER 13, 1945.**

The Luray Caverns in Virginia were discovered on **AUGUST 13, 1878,** when cold air rushed out of a sinkhole on top of a big hill and extinguished a candle held by cave explorer Andrew Campbell.

On Friday, **JULY 13, 1900,** Theodore Roosevelt laid the cornerstone for a new county courthouse in Mineola, New York, and spoke of the need for honesty in government. While he was talking, one man on the platform had his pockets picked of $140, another man lost $103, and several watches were stolen.

On **JUNE 13, 1927,** some 750,000 pounds of paper strips fluttered down around Charles "Lucky Lindy" Lindbergh during a ticker-tape parade in New York City, following his successful completion of the first nonstop, solo flight across the Atlantic Ocean.

On **FEBRUARY 13, 1959,** the first Barbie dolls went on sale.

The Holland Tunnel connecting New York and New Jersey opened on **NOVEMBER 13, 1927.**

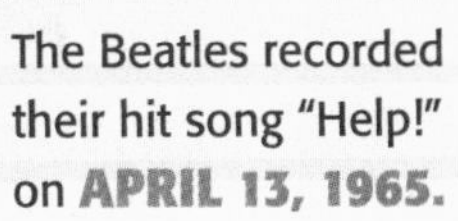

The Beatles recorded their hit song "Help!" on **APRIL 13, 1965.**

Apollo 13 cleared the launch tower at 13:13 (1:13 P.M.) Houston time on April 11, 1970. Two days later—on **APRIL 13**—an oxygen tank in the command module exploded. Thirteen minutes after the explosion, Commander James Lovell noticed that oxygen was escaping from a second tank into space. (After a harrowing 4 days, the crew returned safely to Earth.)

On **JULY 13, 2006,** a Maine fisherman caught a half-brown, half-orange lobster, the odds of catching which are 1 in 50 million.

Hurricane Charley made landfall in Florida on Friday, **AUGUST 13, 2004.**

SPORTS 13s

- **Basketball legend Wilt Chamberlain wore number 13 for the NBA's Philadelphia 76ers and Los Angeles Lakers.**
- **Miami Dolphins quarterback Dan Marino wore number 13.**

continued •••

- Third-baseman Alex Rodriguez wears number **13** for the New York Yankees.

- American swimmer Michael Phelps won his 10th and 11th (out of an eventual total of 14) Olympic gold medals on **August 13, 2008,** in Beijing, China.

WORLDLY 13s

- On many houses in Florence, Italy, $12\frac{1}{2}$ substitutes for **13.**
- A group of French socialites known as quatorziennes (fourteeners) once made themselves available as emergency fill-ins when a dinner party unexpectedly resulted in exactly **13** guests.

- In Great Britain, eating Christmas pudding in **13** different houses before January 1 is supposed to bring joy and prosperity in the next year.
- The traditional New Year's Day in Thailand (Songkran Day) is **April 13.**

FUTURE 13

- Asteroid 99942 Apophis will be closest to Earth on **April 13, 2029.**

Do you have any lucky—or unlucky—**13s?** Share your story or fact at **Almanac4kids.com/TellUs.**

Full Moons

Years ago, Native American tribes assigned names to the full Moon, based on the weather and seasonal events. Some of these names are still used today.

JANUARY	FEBRUARY	MARCH	APRIL
When the Snow Blows Like Spirits in the Wind Moon (Northern Arapaho)	Shoulder to Shoulder Around the Fire Moon (Wishram)	Moon When Eyes Are Sore From Bright Snow (Lakota Sioux)	Moon When the Geese Lay Eggs (Cheyenne)
MAY	**JUNE**	**JULY**	**AUGUST**
Season When the Leaves Are Green Moon (Apache)	Full Leaf Moon (Assiniboine)	Ripe Corn Moon (Cherokee)	Moon When the Geese Shed Their Feathers (Lakota Sioux)

SEPTEMBER	OCTOBER	NOVEMBER	DECEMBER
Moon When the Plums Are Scarlet (Lakota Sioux)	Moon When the Water Begins to Freeze on the Edge of the Streams (Cheyenne)	Snowy Mountains in the Morning Moon (Wishram)	Turning Moon (Zuni)

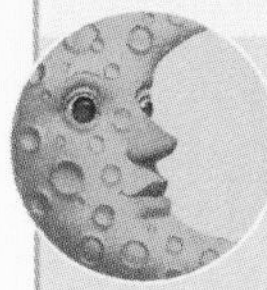

The Moon and YOU! Create a list of full Moon names, based on natural events, your favorite things to do, or your family traditions. Share your Moon names at **Almanac4kids.com/TellUs.**

February's 400-Year Cycle

YEARS in which February contains five Sundays occur 13 times every 400 years at specific intervals. The order of the intervals is as follows:

- **three 28-year intervals**
- **one 40-year interval**
- **two 28-year intervals**
- **one 40-year interval**
- **two 28-year intervals**
- **one 40 years interval**
- **three 28-year intervals**

The last year in which February had five Sundays was 2004. Which of the next 400 years will have five Sundays in February? (Hint: Add the interval periods to 2004. Answer below.)

FIVE-SUNDAY FEBRUARY FACTS:

- **Years with five Sundays in February are leap years.**
- **January 1 in these years falls on a Thursday.**
- **February 1 in these years falls on a Sunday.**

How do you know if it's a LEAP YEAR?

1. Leap years are exactly divisible by 4. However, years ending in 00 are leap years only when they are exactly divisible by 400. (For example, 2000 is but 1900 is not).
2. "Leapless" years begin and end on the same day of the week.

ANSWER: 2032, 2060, 2088, 2128, 2156, 2184, 2224, 2252, 2280, 2320, 2348, 2376, 2404

Arbor Day, ROOTS AND ALL!

Julius Sterling Morton

n April 22, 1885, every student (about 1,000 total) in Nebraska City, Nebraska, planted at least one tree. To each tree, the students attached a tag noting the time, their school and grade, and instructions for care of the tree. Then the children, many of whom carried a banner, paraded to the opera house. Along the way, about 1,000 adults joined them. As the marchers filed into the building, the children took seats while the adults stood. All were assembled to hear the man who had inspired the plantings, Julius Sterling Morton. It was his birthday and, in his honor, the first (official) Arbor Day.

Julius had dreamed up the idea of Arbor Day in 1854, when he and his wife, Caroline Joy, moved from Michigan to the Nebraska Territory. (The area became a state in 1867.) At that time, few trees grew there, and Julius became determined to change that. He bought land for a homestead and began planting trees on it. Then he

Students paraded to the opera house. Along the way, about 1,000 adults joined them. Everyone wanted to hear Julius Sterling Morton speak.

planted trees wherever and whenever he could. Over his lifetime, he planted thousands of trees that became orchards and forests.

Getting other people in the community involved had not always been easy. Julius had planned the first Arbor Day for April 10, 1872. He had ordered 800 trees but then had to cancel the event when the trees did not arrive in time.

As editor of a newspaper, Julius wrote about the importance of trees: They keep soil in place, are burned for fuel, are used to build homes, and provide protection from the Sun. He also gave speeches about the benefits and beauty of trees.

Nebraska governor Robert W. Furnas proclaimed April 10, 1874, as Arbor Day. In 1885, it became a legal holiday in Nebraska.

Today, Arbor Day is celebrated around the world. In most of the United States, it is the last Friday in April. Some states observe it on different dates to coincide with best planting times.

Arbor Day is celebrated in some Canadian provinces, but across the country, people celebrate Maple Leaf Day on the last Wednesday in September, during National Forest Week.

READ THE RINGS

Dendrochronology is the study of tree rings. These rings reveal a tree's age and are visible in a trunk when a tree is cut horizontally.

Many trees produce rings, including conifers, aspen, beech, maple, and oak. All have these layers:

- **outer skin, or BARK protects the tree**
- **PHLOEM, or inner bark, carries food from the leaves to the rest of the tree**
- **CAMBIUM produces new bark and new wood**
- **XYLEM, or sapwood, brings water and nutrients from the roots to the leaves**
- **HEARTWOOD, or old xylem, gives the tree support**

A ring is formed when a tree adds a layer of xylem cells. One ring equals 1 year of a tree's life. Narrow rings indicate dry weather years, while wide rings indicate rainy years. Light-color rings indicate spring growth, while dark rings indicate summer growth.

THAT'S OLD!

- **A white cedar tree on the Niagara Escarpment in Ontario was estimated to be 1,630 years old in 2010.**

- **The roots of a "Christmas tree" conifer found in Sweden have been determined to be 9,550 years old. The tree's trunk lives for about 600 years; when it dies, the roots send up a new one.**

- **A Great Basin bristlecone pine nicknamed Methuselah in California's Inyo National Forest was estimated to be 4,842 years old in 2010. Its exact location is a secret so that no one will disturb it.**

Happy
RIP

Halloween!

TRICKS and TREATS for GHOULS and BOILS

A Howling History of October 31

Centuries ago, this was a 2-day celebration that marked the end of harvesttime and the beginning of the new year.

- At night, people put food outside on the doorstep for evil spirits who might otherwise play a trick on them. People wore costumes outdoors at night and made lots of noise to scare away evil spirits.
- "Witch" originally meant "wise one." People thought that witches told fortunes and flew out of chimneys on broomsticks.
- Ancient Romans bobbed for apples, believing that the first person to catch an apple with his or her teeth would be the first to marry in the new year.
- In ancient Ireland, people carved faces in turnips and potatoes and beets—not pumpkins.
- "Trick or treating" dates from the Middle Ages, when rich people gave poor people "soul cakes" (baked goods) if they promised to pray for the giver's dead family members.

continued

Get Scary

Paint Your Face

FOR EACH PAINT COLOR, YOU WILL NEED:

paper cup
1 teaspoon cornstarch
½ teaspoon cold cream
½ teaspoon water
1 to 2 drops food coloring
small paintbrush or cotton swab

Put the cornstarch and cold cream into a paper cup and mix until blended. Add the water and food coloring, then stir. Use a paintbrush or swab to apply the paint to your face. Remove with soap and water.

Bleed With Fake Blood

YOU WILL NEED:

1 cup light corn syrup
1 teaspoon red food coloring

Combine the ingredients in a bowl and stir to blend. Add water, a few drops at time, if the mixture is too thick, then stir. Apply the "blood" to your clothes and body. (Food coloring can stain fabric permanently, so wear old clothing.)

Do a Monster Makeover

YOU WILL NEED:

3 tablespoons cornstarch
1 tablespoon flour
¾ cup light corn syrup
¼ cup water
4 paper cups
3 food colorings
tissue paper, torn lengthwise into 2-inch strips
puffed wheat cereal

In a bowl, mix together the cornstarch and flour. Add the corn syrup and water and stir until smooth. Divide the mixture into four paper cups. Add one food coloring to each of three cups. Stir each one. Keep the fourth mixture untinted.

For "skin": Paint some untinted mixture onto a section of your face. Place strips of tissue paper over it. Cover with more untinted mixture. Continue covering your face, one area at a time.

For "warts": Stick puffed wheat to the untinted mixture on your face and cover with tissue paper.

For fun: When the mixture on your face is dry, use the colored mixtures to paint your face.

To remove, wet your face and peel the tissue away. Wash your face with soap and water.

Wear an Orange-skin Grin

YOU WILL NEED:

1 orange
paring knife
food coloring, optional

Cut the orange into four equal wedges. Remove and save the peels from two. (Eat the fruit!) Turn the peels inside out. Cut a row of ugly teeth along one edge of each peel to make upper and lower teeth. (Ask an adult to help, if necessary.) Paint the teeth with food coloring, if desired. Put the peels under your lips and over your teeth. Cut away some of the peel from the toothless edges, if needed, to make them fit.

What subject do witches like best?

Spelling.

continued

SNEAKY SNACKS

Egg-oogily Eyes

YOU WILL NEED:

1 hard-boiled egg, shell removed
mayonnaise
food coloring (blue, green, or red)
1 pimiento-stuffed green olive, sliced in half
cotton swab (optional)

Cut the egg in half lengthwise. Remove the yolk from each half. In a small bowl, mix the yolk with a spoonful of mayonnaise. Add one or two drops of food coloring and stir to blend. Place the egg white halves on a plate. Mound a spoonful of colored yolk on each half and use your fingers to give it a round shape. Push the rounded end of an olive half into each yolk. For bloodshot eyes, use a cotton swab and red food coloring to paint blood vessels on the egg whites. MAKES 2 PER EGG.

Slippery Worm Sandwich

YOU WILL NEED:

hot dogs
barbecue sauce or ketchup
sandwich buns

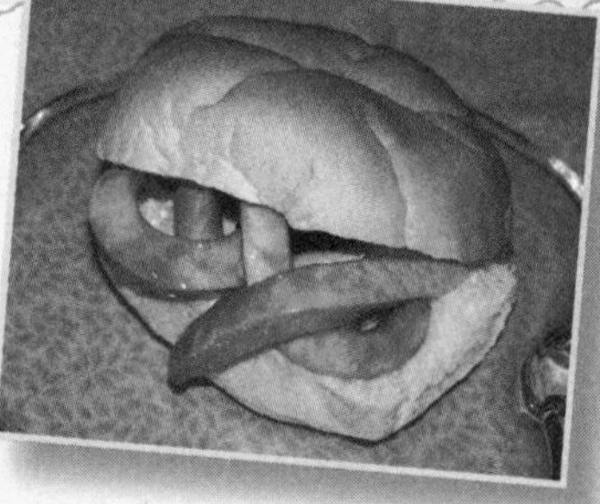

Ask an adult to help: Slice the hot dogs, cutting them in half lengthwise and then in half lengthwise again. Carefully place the hot dog strips in a pot of boiling water. Cook for 1 to 2 minutes, or until they begin to curl. Use tongs to remove the strips from the water and set them aside on a paper towel to drain and cool. Put the strips into a bowl. Add barbecue sauce and stir to coat. Serve on buns. **MAKES 1 SANDWICH PER HOT DOG.**

Q. How do you mend a broken jack-o'-lantern?
A. **With a pumpkin patch.**

Mouthy Munchies

YOU WILL NEED:

1 apple
slivered almonds
toothpicks
miniature marshmallows

Quarter the apple. On the skin side, cut out a wedge, without slicing through to the core. Push almond pieces into the top and bottom portions of the wedge cuts. Break a toothpick in half and stick each half into the top of an apple section. Push a marshmallow onto each toothpick. **MAKES 4 PER APPLE.**

Cookie Critters

YOU WILL NEED:

black licorice, cut into 1-inch-long pieces
chocolate sandwich cookies
chocolate frosting
miniature chocolate-coated candies

Take six to eight pieces of licorice (depending on the size of the cookies) and push them into the sides of each cookie. Dab a small amount of chocolate frosting on two miniature chocolate-coated candies and stick them on the cookie to look like eyes. **MAKES 1 CRITTER PER COOKIE.**

LIGHT FOR FRIGHT

YOU WILL NEED:

3 or 4 plastic 1-gallon milk jugs, cleaned
permanent markers
scissors or a paring knife
strings of holiday lights

Draw a ghost face on one side of each jug. Ask an adult to cut a 1½-inch hole in the back of the jug for the lights. Push a few lights into each jug. Display the jugs in a group inside (with the room lights off, for best effect) or outside at night, if the lights are suitable for outdoor use.

Give Thanks to Sarah Josepha Hale

Without her, we wouldn't have Thanksgiving Day.

Sarah Josepha Buell was born on October 24, 1788, on a farm in Newport, New Hampshire. From a tender age, she was curious, smart, and eager to learn.

As a young girl, Sarah was taught by her mother about history and literature. Later, her brother Horatio taught her everything that he was learning as a student at Dartmouth College.

When Sarah was growing up, women were not accepted as teachers. However, this didn't stop her from founding a private school when she was 18 years old. She taught until she met David Hale. They married in 1813.

David encouraged Sarah to write short stories and articles. Many of these were published in local newspapers.

Suddenly, in 1822, David died, and Sarah was left to care for their five children. To make ends meet, she first operated a women's hat shop and later resumed teaching and writing. Soon she published her first book of poems, including one that became the famous nursery rhyme "Mary Had a Little Lamb." In 1827, she published her first novel.

John Blake of Boston read Sarah's novel and asked her to work for him on *Ladies' Magazine.* Sarah accepted and became the first woman editor of a magazine in the United States. She introduced new ideas and a new title, calling it *American Ladies' Magazine.*

Within a few years, Louis Godey of Philadelphia bought John's magazine and merged it with *Godey's Lady's Book,* keeping Sarah as editor.

Throughout this period, Sarah had written hundreds of letters to governors, ministers, newspaper editors, and every U.S. president with one request: that the last Thursday in November be set aside to "offer to God our tribute of joy and gratitude for the blessings of the year."

Native American harvest festivals and colonists' services to give thanks had taken place for centuries in North America, but there was no one Thanksgiving holiday.

In 1863, with the country torn by the Civil War, Sarah's idea finally got people's attention. That September, she put her thanksgiving message into an editorial and wrote to President Abraham Lincoln, urging him to make Thanksgiving Day a fixed national festival.

Lincoln liked Sarah's idea. On October 3, 1863, he issued a proclamation declaring the last Thursday of November to be National Thanksgiving Day. He ordered all government offices in Washington closed on that day.

Sarah enjoyed many Thanksgiving celebrations. She died on April 30, 1879, at the age of 90.

Finally, the Fourth

IN 1939, President Franklin Roosevelt was pressured by store owners to move Thanksgiving Day to the third Thursday in November. They wanted more shopping days between Thanksgiving and Christmas. He did it, but millions of Americans continued to celebrate Thanksgiving Day on the last Thursday of November.

In 1940, President Roosevelt realized his mistake. In the spring of 1941, he assigned the holiday to the fourth Thursday in November.

How About Monday?

Occasions for thanksgiving in Canada have been observed for hundreds of years. Thanksgiving became a national holiday in 1879; its date each year was determined by proclamation. In 1957, Parliament set the second Monday in October as the fixed date "for general thanksgiving to Almighty God for the blessings with which the people of Canada have been favoured."

Decembers to Firsts in the

Christmas Firsts

1535 The first **Christmas in Canada** was observed by Jacques Cartier and 110 settlers on the banks of the St. Charles River near the city of Quebec.

1539 The first **Christmas in the continental United States** was observed by Hernando de Soto and his 600-member expedition near what is now Tallahassee, Florida.

1776 The first North American **Christmas tree** was set up by Henrick Roddmore, a German soldier who was captured in the Revolutionary War's Battle of Bennington (Vermont).

1851 The first **Christmas tree sales lot** in the United States was set up by Mark Carr of Pennsylvania. He brought two sleds, each full of cut trees and pulled by oxen, from the Catskill Mountains to the sidewalks of New York City.

1856 The first U.S. president to set up a **Christmas tree in the White House** was Franklin Pierce.

1875 The first North American **Christmas cards** were printed and sold by Louis Prang of Roxbury, Massachusetts.

1923 The first U.S. president to establish the **National Tree Lighting Ceremony** on the grounds of the White House was Calvin Coolidge.

1890 The first **department store Santa Claus** was James Edgar, who, during Christmas seasons, would wander about his store (the Boston Store) in Brockton, Massachusetts, dressed as Santa Claus, talking to the children of customers.

1898 The first **Christmas postage stamp** was released in Canada on December 7. It cost 2 cents and bore the words "XMAS 1898" as well as an image of the Mercator (projection) world map.

Remember last month of the year

Chanukah Firsts

The **FIRST DAY** of the 8 days **OF CHANUKAH,** the festival of lights, is the 25th day of the Jewish month of Kislev. On the Gregorian calendar, this date almost always falls in late November or early December.

"Chanukah" comes from the Hebrew word for "dedicate." This festival was **FIRST CELEBRATED** around 165 B.C., to commemorate the rededication of a temple at which a day's worth of lamp oil miraculously burned for 8 days.

The candles on the menorah are lit from right to left, **ONE FOR EACH DAY** of the festival.

Kwanzaa Firsts

- **This African and African-American holiday period, from December 26 through January 1, was FIRST CELEBRATED in 1966.**
- **Every day for seven days, a candle is lit to celebrate Kwanzaa's seven principles. The FIRST CANDLE is black; the FIRST PRINCIPLE is unity.**
- **"Kwanzaa" comes from the Swahili phrase for "FIRST FRUITS" *(matunda ya kwanza)* and is a celebration of family, community, and culture.**
- **The FIRST KWANZAA U.S. POSTAGE STAMP, with artwork by Synthia Saint James, was issued on October 22, 1997.**

Oh, My Hea

Wonders of the night sky to watch for throughout the year

vens!

Gases and dust from star formation around the M17 nebula are revealed in this infrared image from NASA's Spitzer Space Telescope.

(turn the page to begin)

Winter

More bright stars are on display in winter than during any other time of the year. On the clearest night in the darkest place, about 3,000 stars are visible to the naked eye.

BETELGEUSE, the largest star visible to the naked eye, resides in the constellation ORION, which was originally a sheep, not a hunter. This famous red star's name means "sheep's armpit."

Sirius

Betelgeuse

The CRAB NEBULA *(right)*, in the Taurus constellation, is a giant gas cloud made up of the remnants of a star that "went supernova," or blew up, in 1054. The explosion was so bright that it could be seen during daylight hours for weeks. Today, a 12-mile-wide pulsar star spins at the center of the Crab Nebula, flashing 30 times per second. The energy released from this wild rotation lights up the entire cloud, making it visible with a telescope.

Polaris

Spring

The BIG DIPPER reaches its highest place in the sky in spring. Look for its two pointer stars on the outer side of its bowl aiming toward POLARIS, the North Star. Take note: The North

Pleiades star cluster

Above, a fireball meteor speeds through the constellation Orion and lights up the Mojave Desert during a Geminid meteor shower in December.

Star is not the brightest star in the sky. Forty-five other stars are brighter. Polaris is the only star that doesn't appear to move.

The most crowded part of the night sky is also the darkest. Halfway up the southern sky is the constellation VIRGO. It is identified by the bright-blue star SPICA, above which (65 million light-years from Earth) lurks the VIRGO CLUSTER, containing thousands of galaxies. Through backyard telescopes, these galaxies look like gray blobs; they are invisible to the naked eye.

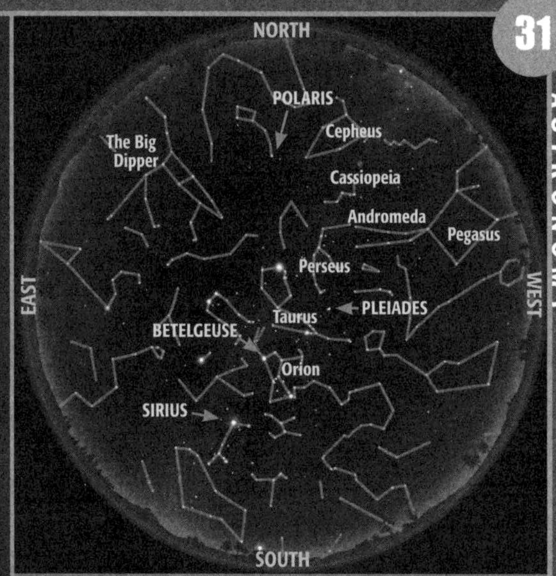

WINTER CONSTELLATIONS

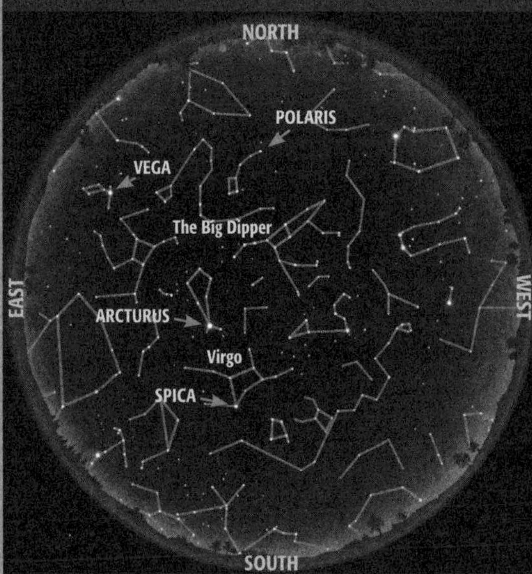

SPRING CONSTELLATIONS

These star charts show the view from the mid–Northern Hemisphere. The outer edge of the circles is the closest to the horizon, while the center of the circle shows the night sky directly overhead.

(turn the page for more)

Summer

In early summer, blue-white star VEGA and orange star ARCTURUS are both bright and high in the night sky. Peering lower, you can see several white, orange, and blue stars.

The season's most popular stargazing night is August 11–12, when the PERSEID METEORS blaze across the sky. Usually, on a clear night, one meteor per minute can be seen after midnight. All are actually 50 to 100 miles overhead and all move at exactly 37 miles per second.

Moonless nights in summer offer the year's best views of the thickest part of our galaxy, the MILKY WAY. In dark, rural regions, it dominates the sky. Look for a hazy, white band of light, with the brightest portion near the southern horizon.

NASA's Hubble Space Telescope, Spitzer Space Telescope, and Chandra X-ray Observatory produced this image of our Milky Way Galaxy, the center of which is the light at the right. The bright white light at the left is an X-ray binary star.

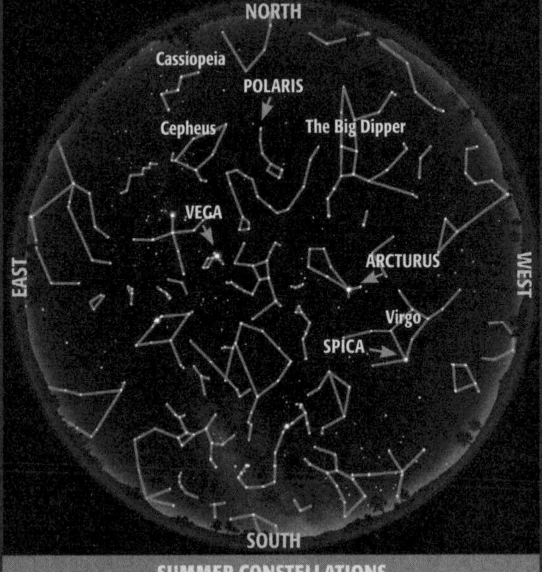

SUMMER CONSTELLATIONS

These star charts show the view from the mid-Northern Hemisphere. The outer edge of the circles is the closest to the horizon, while the center of the circle shows the night sky directly overhead.

Autumn

Can you name the most distant object visible to the naked eye? It's the ANDROMEDA GALAXY. About 2.5 million light-years away, it appears as a faint oval blob, almost directly above much of the United States and Canada. The glow that we see comes from 1 trillion stars.

The constellations PERSEUS, PEGASUS, ANDROMEDA, CEPHEUS, and CASSIOPEIA all appear on high now, yet none contains a first-magnitude star. Most of the stars of these famous legends in Greek mythology are of medium or fainter brightness.

The most famous star cluster is the PLEIADES, or Seven Sisters, but who's counting? Average eyesight sees six stars. Superb vision reveals 8 to 11 stars. Nobody sees exactly seven. No matter. This concentration of young blue stars is the finest sight through binoculars in all of the heavens.

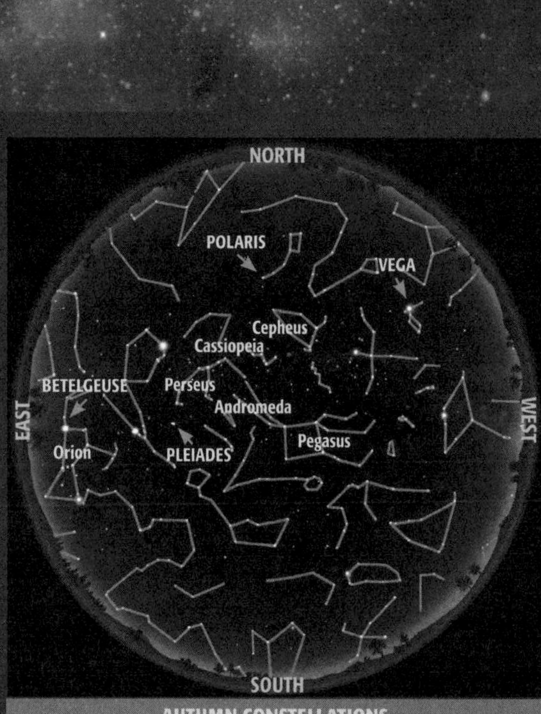

AUTUMN CONSTELLATIONS

Star Light, HOW BRIGHT?

Star brightness is called magnitude. The lower the magnitude number, the brighter the star. On a clear night, away from city lights and with binoculars, we can see stars that are a faint magnitude 6 or 7. On a clear night in a city or suburb, we can see stars of magnitude 2, 3, or 4 with the naked eye. HERE ARE SOME RELATIVE EXAMPLES:

YOU CAN SEE . . .	MAGNITUDE	WITH . . .
Sun	–26	eye protection; viewing not recommended without it
full Moon	–13	naked eye
crescent Moon	–6	naked eye
Venus	–4	naked eye
Jupiter	–2	naked eye
Sirius (star)	–1	naked eye
Vega (star)	0	naked eye
Saturn	+1	naked eye (best in dark, rural areas)
Big Dipper (stars)	+2	naked eye
Andromeda Galaxy	+3 or +4	naked eye
moons of Jupiter	+5	binoculars
Uranus	+6	binoculars
bright asteroids	+7	binoculars
Neptune	+8	telescope
some comets	+10 to +13	telescope
Pluto, at its brightest	+14	telescope

Sirius-ly! It's the DOG STAR

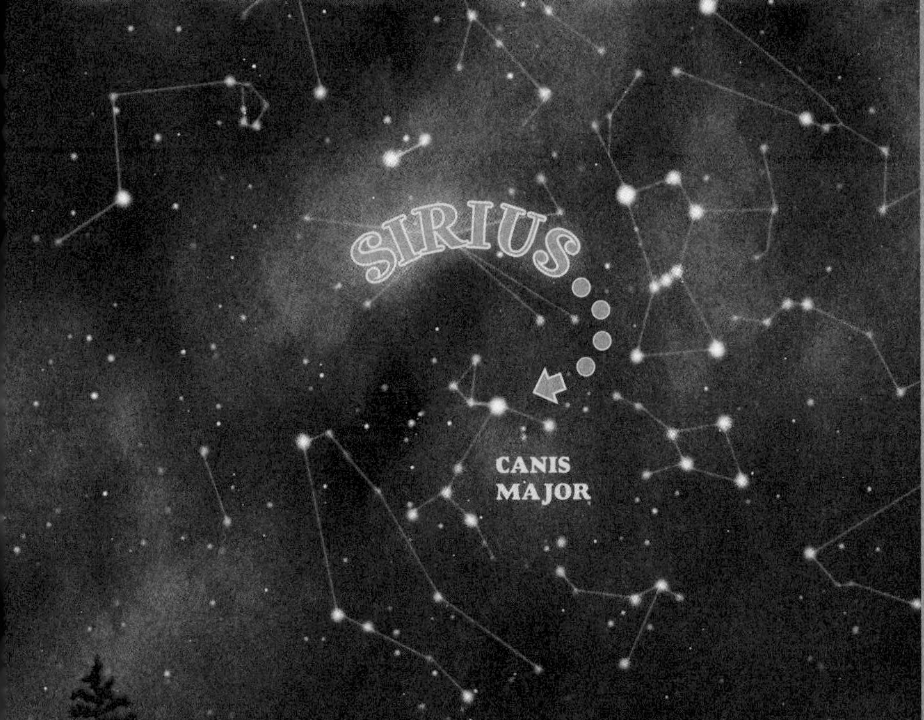

SIRIUS

CANIS MAJOR

Sirius is the brightest star in the sky, if you don't count the Sun. Under the right conditions, it can even be seen with the naked eye during the day. Sirius is one star in a group of stars that form the constellation Canis Major, meaning "Greater Dog." It's no surprise, then, that the nickname of this big, bold star is Dog Star.

★ (continued)

"SOTHIS" Is It

- The Egyptians named this bright star SOTHIS. The Greeks called it Sirius, meaning "scorching."
- Its appearance in the sky just prior to that of the Sun is called a "heliacal" rising.
- Sirius has a brightness, or magnitude, of –1.4. (It is one of only four stars of negative magnitude. To learn more about star brightness, turn to page 34.)

Sirius-ly WET

- In ancient Egypt, the Nile River flooded each year, usually beginning in late June. The people welcomed this event, called the Inundation, because the floodwaters brought rich soil needed to grow crops in what was otherwise a desert.
- No one in Egypt knew exactly when the flooding would start, but they noticed a coincidence that gave them a clue: The waters began to rise on the days when Sirius began to rise before the Sun.
- Sirius and the Inundation became so important to the Egyptians' survival that they began their new year with the new Moon that followed the star's first appearance on the eastern horizon.

Sirius-ly HOT

- Unlike the Egyptians, the ancient Greeks and Romans were not pleased by Sirius's appearance. For them, Sirius signaled the beginning of the hot season, which brought

SIRIUS-LY LATE

Due to a very slow wobble of Earth's axis, the Dog Star now seems to rise later than it did in ancient times. Its ascension no longer coincides with the start of the Nile flood (which does not occur anyway, because the river is now controlled by the Aswan Dam), but Sirius still makes its appearance during hot summer days.

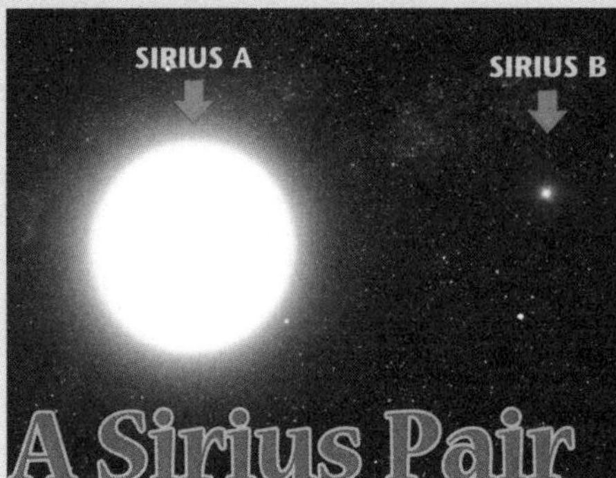

A Sirius Pair

The Dog Star is not alone. Sirius and another star close by are in orbit around a common center. Sirius A, the Dog Star, is the bigger, brighter star of the pair. Sirius B is the companion star, sometimes called the "Pup."

UNLUCKY DOG DAYS

Old-timers believed that rainfall on the dog days was a bad omen, as foretold in this verse:

Dog days bright
and clear
Indicate a happy year;
But when accompanied
by rain,
For better times, our
hopes
are vain.

drought, disease, and discomfort. Some people believed that the summer swelter was due to the combined heat from Sirius and the Sun. These uncomfortable, unhealthy days were called the dog days, named after the (innocent) Dog Star.

Traditionally, the dog days last for 40 days, beginning on July 3 and ending on August 11.

Look Out. BE-LOW-W FOR METEORITES!

A **meteoroid** is a small piece of stony, metallic, or icy matter that hurtles through space.

A **meteor** is a meteoroid that enters Earth's atmosphere and briefly streaks across the sky.

A **meteorite** is a meteor that lands on the surface of Earth or another celestial body.

A **comet** is a chunk of icy dust that often has a tail. Although it is orbiting the Sun, it appears to hover in the night sky.

Every second, about 10 **meteoroids** enter Earth's atmosphere. Friction from the air heats them up and causes bright streaks of light that can last from a second to several minutes. These are also called falling stars or shooting stars. If one is extremely bright, it is called a fireball.

Most meteoroids disintegrate in Earth's atmosphere. They create an estimated 1,000 to 10,0000 tons of meteorite "material" that enters Earth's atmosphere each day. Most of these particles are dustlike and fall gently and harmlessly.

Meteorites usually weigh more than Earth rocks of the same size because they have a higher nickel-iron content. They are also older. The longer a meteorite is on Earth, the more its glassy crust wears away, leaving the meteorite a rusty brown color.

Comets are icy bodies (think of dirty snowballs). When a comet's orbit brings it close enough to the Sun, some of its ice melts, making water vapor and dust particles fly off of it and creating a tail.

Comet Kohoutek was discovered on March 7, 1973, by Czech astronomer Luboš Kohoutek.

CONTINUED

What are the odds of being hit by a meteorite?

Most meteors fall in uninhabited parts of the world—but not all of them. Scientists at the Herzberg Institute of Astrophysics in Ottawa, Canada, made these calculations after using 60 cameras to study meteor falls for 9 years:

- Someone in North America will be struck by a piece of cosmic debris once every 180 years, on average.
- Worldwide, a human might be struck once every 9 years.
- About 16 buildings a year might be damaged by meteorites.

A Trio of True Tales

1 An Unscheduled Visit

On January 18, 2010, Frank Ciampi, a doctor in Lorton, Virginia, was in his office when he heard a loud boom. Then he noticed a hole in the ceiling and three small chunks of rock, plus four or five tinier pieces, that had landed about 10 feet away from him.

A planetary scientist confirmed that the rock was a meteorite and determined that it had been traveling at about 220 mph when it hit the building.

All together, the rocks are about the size of a tennis ball and weigh just over half a pound.

2 Eliza Knew Best

The farm fields in Brenham, Kansas, are flat, without many rocks. However, in the 1880s farmers kept hitting metallic rocks with their plows. Eliza Kimberly noticed that these rocks were like a meteorite she had seen as a child in Iowa. Over 5 years, she wrote letters to scientists, trying to convince them to study the rocks in Brenham.

Finally they did, and Eliza was right. These rocks were part of a meteorite (now called the Brenham meteorite) that scattered more than 3 tons of fragments on the town's farmlands.

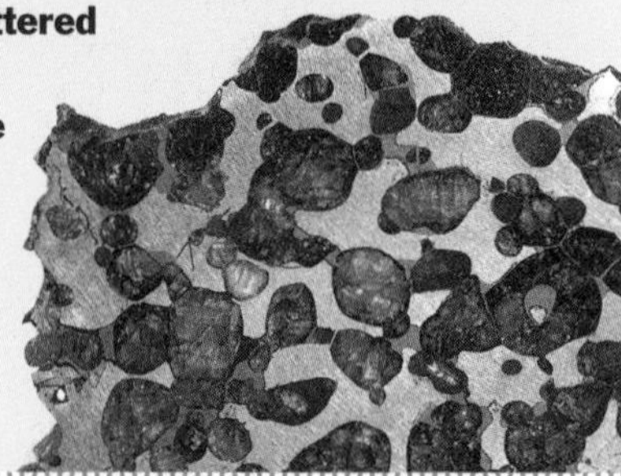

A polished piece of the Brenham meteorite

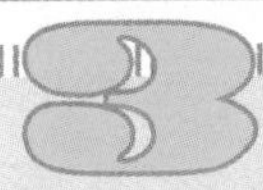

THE SNOOZE THAT MADE NEWS

The only confirmed case of a meteorite actually hitting a human occurred on November 30, 1954, in Sylacauga, Alabama, not far from a restaurant called—of all things—the Comet Drive-In.

Ann Hodges, age 31, was napping on her couch. She woke up when a meteorite crashed through the roof, smashed a wooden radio cabinet, and then hit her hand and hip, causing terrible bruising. At first, Ann thought that her space heater had exploded. When she saw the rock, she thought that some mischievous children had been up to no good.

The event caused great excitement: The police and the mayor were called, and reporters and sightseers soon filled Ann's yard. An inspection team arrived aboard a helicopter, and Air Force specialists confirmed that this was an 8½-pound meteorite. A smaller fragment was discovered about 2 miles from the Hodges home.

The Hodges meteorite is on display at the Alabama Museum of Natural History in Tuscaloosa.

SPECIAL DELIVERY

- A mailbox that was hit by a meteorite in Claxton, Georgia, sold for nearly $83,000.

CONTINUED

WEATHER OR NOT?

For thousands of years, meteorites have been picked up and even worshipped. Natives used them for iron tools and jewelry. People thought that they came from volcanoes or hurricanes or resulted from lightning strikes.

In 1794, German physicist **Ernst Chladni** published a book in which he claimed that iron and rock specimens fall from the sky and produce fireballs and that they must be from space. Many people laughed at this idea, but today Chladni is considered the founder of "meteoritics," the study of meteorites. ("Meteorology," which refers to the study of weather in the atmosphere, had already been taken.)

Today, there are about 27,000 meteorites in collections around the world. The Smithsonian Institution in Washington, D.C., has about half of these.

FOUND:

On Mars and the Moon

- The Mars rover *Opportunity* found a basketball-size meteorite in January 2005. Scientists call it Heat Shield Rock because it was found near the rover's abandoned heat shield.
- During *Apollo* missions, two meteorites—Bench Crater and Hadley Rille, named for nearby craters—were found on the Moon.

A WHOLE LOT OF HOLE

Meteor Crater, near Winslow, Arizona, is 2.4 miles in circumference, nearly 1 mile across, and more than 550 feet deep. Scientists believe that about 50,000 years ago, a meteoroid about 150 feet across landed here at a speed of about 26,000 mph. The impact of the crash caused some of the rock to vaporize, melt, and break into pieces. It also blasted out over 175 million tons of limestone and sandstone, which formed a continuous layer of debris surrounding the crater for a distance of over a mile.

THE BIGGEST EVER

In 1920, a farmer in Grootfontein, Namibia, was plowing his field with his ox when his plow became stuck. He began digging and discovered a massive rock. A scientist named Jacobus Hermanus Brits later identified the rock as the largest known meteorite on Earth.

The meteorite is so heavy (an estimated 60 tons) that it has never been moved, although pieces have been removed for study and sometimes, sadly, for souvenirs.

Scientists named the meteorite after the place where it was discovered—Farm Hoba West. Experts estimate that the Hoba meteorite landed about 80,000 years ago, at a low angle, skipping along Earth's surface like a stone on water. (That's why it did not cause a crater.)

Don't Miss the Shower

Meteor showers occur when Earth's orbit takes our planet near where millions of particles have fallen off comets. These showers are named after the constellations from which the meteors appear to fall. Two of the best-known meteor showers are the Perseids, which peak on August 11, 12, and 13, and the Geminids, which peak on December 13 and 14.

HOW AND WHEN TO WATCH

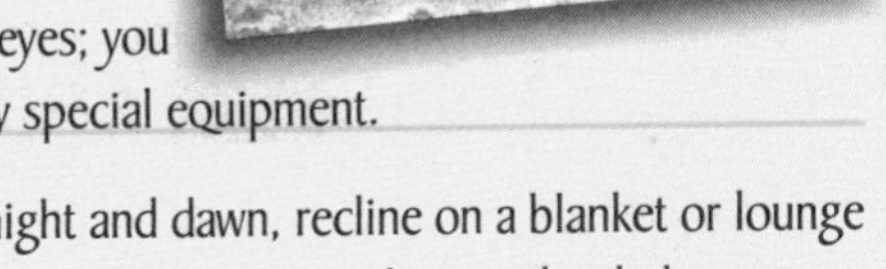

Find a dark area, away from bright lights.

Use just your eyes; you don't need any special equipment.

Between midnight and dawn, recline on a blanket or lounge chair and look up. Let your eyes adjust to the darkness.

Meteors are fast, and they sneak across the sky when you least expect them. On a clear night, you can often see one streaking by about once every 1 to 5 minutes.

CALLING ALL ALIENS

Flying saucers?

Little green men?

UFOs?

The search for

extraterrestrial life

goes on.

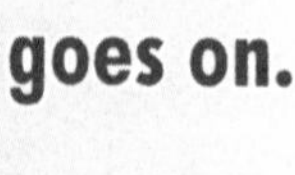

The first unidentified flying object (UFO) sightings in North America were made around January 18, 1644. Massachusetts Bay Colony governor John Winthrop documented the occurrence in his journal.

An artist's rendering of a quasar (bright center of a young star)

The science of the search for intelligent life in outer space is called **astrobiology.** It brings together many different disciplines, including . . .

- **astronomy**
- **astrophysics**
- **cosmochemistry**
- **Earth and planetary sciences**
- **biology**
- **microbiology**

CONTINUED

The Goldilocks Zone Is Just Right

An artist's rendering of the Kepler spacecraft

On March 6, 2009, NASA launched a spacecraft aboard a rocket from Cape Canaveral in Florida as part of a project called the Kepler Mission. The spacecraft contains the largest telescope ever sent beyond Earth's orbit. It can monitor more than 100,000 stars every half hour.

The mission, which will last between 3½ and 6 years, has two main goals:

- **to find planets in our own Milky Way galaxy that are close to Earth's size and might be able to support liquid water and life**
- **to determine how many of the billions of stars in our galaxy have such planets**

Before this project began, more than 300 "extrasolar" planetary bodies were known to exist. Scientists look in the "Goldilocks zone," where it is "not too hot and not too cold" to support life, thanks to each planet's distance from its parent star.

TRUE BELIEVERS

Around 1900, in his Colorado Springs laboratory, inventor **Nikola Tesla** received what he believed to be a signal from outer space. People laughed, but he was possibly the first person to detect radio signals from space.

- In 1920, Italian inventor **Guglielmo Marconi** used early radio technology to try to hear signals from space.

- About 1950, Nobel Prize–winning physicist **Enrico Fermi** began believing that alien civilizations were likely to exist, but he wondered why there were no verified stories of extraterrestrial visits to Earth. He asked: Why haven't we seen any? His question became known as the Fermi Paradox.

In 1961, a radio astronomer named Dr. Frank Drake created the Drake Equation, a mathematical formula for calculating the possible number of extraterrestrial civilizations in the MILKY WAY. By his estimate, there are likely to be 10,000 communicating civilizations—and that's just in our galaxy!

Dust lanes, bright nebulae, and star clusters within the central Milky Way

Hello, Out There!

People have *tried* to communicate to aliens . . .

In the 1800s, some people wanted to clear large stretches of Siberian forest so that, from the sky, the openings would "spell out" the mathematical Pythagorean theorem.

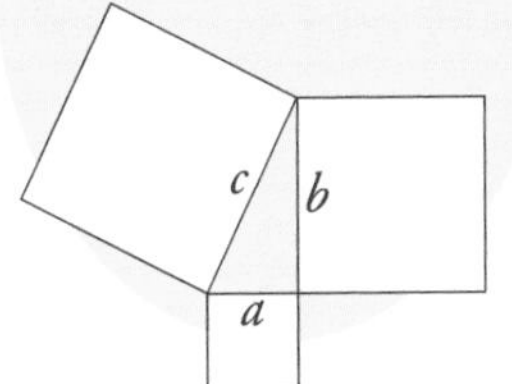

At about the same time, someone else wanted to dig trenches in different geometric shapes in the Sahara Desert, fill them with kerosene, and light them. (Neither this nor the tree clearing idea was implemented.)

CONTINUED

In 1974, the ARECIBO BROADCAST, the most powerful broadcast ever made, was sent from a radio telescope in Puerto Rico. The message lasted less than 3 minutes and contained 1,679 bits of data that formed simple images representing (among other things) the telescope itself, the solar system, a stick figure of a human, and information about DNA. The broadcast was aimed at a star cluster called M13, which is about 25,000 light-years away and contains about 300,000 stars.

In 1977, 12-inch GOLD-PLATED COPPER DISKS were launched into space aboard NASA's *Voyager I* and *Voyager II*. The *Voyager* Golden Records contained sounds and images intended to communicate to aliens what life is like on Earth.

Other broadcast messages were "COSMIC CALL" (in 1999 and 2003) from the Ukraine and the "TEENAGE MESSAGE," put together by Russian teens in 2001.

One Big "WOW"

On August 15, 1977, an unusual burst of radio noise got the attention of astronomer Jerry Ehman, who was on duty at the **Big Ear Radio Observatory** at The Ohio State University.

The signal lasted 37 seconds and came from the direction of the nearest star, some 220 light-years away! Strangely, the noise traveled on a frequency whose use is prohibited by international agreement and that is unlike those of most natural radio sources.

When Dr. Ehman noticed the signal, he wrote "Wow" next to it on the paper printout, and since then it has been called the Wow signal. Scientists have searched for another signal like it but have never found one.

BASE OF OPERATIONS

Scientists at the SETI (Search for Extra-Terrestrial Intelligence) Institute in Mountain View, California, have one assignment: Find aliens. One of their major projects is the **Allen Telescope Array.** The array is being built at the Hat Creek Radio Observatory, about 300 miles northeast of San Francisco. Currently, there are 42 working telescopes in place. Eventually, there will be 350, each shaped like a 20-foot-wide satellite dish.

When they have adequate funding, scientists will be able to search for alien communication sent by advanced civilizations in our own and other galaxies and conduct astronomical research at the same time.

THE LARGEST TELESCOPE IN NORTH AMERICA devoted to SETI is located at the **Oak Ridge Observatory** in Harvard, Massachusetts. Equipped with a 72-inch mirror and in use since 2006, it is known as the first all-sky Optical SETI (OSETI).

Observers have noted dozens of interesting light pulses through its lenses, but so far scientists have concluded that none were sent from extraterrestrial beings.

TALK TO ALIENS (and Each Other)

Do you think that there is intelligent life in outer space? What would you say to an alien? Share your messages with other kids (and possibly aliens!) at **Almanac4kids.com/TellUs.**

Rise and Shine

How Does the Sun Rise and Set?

It doesn't. The Sun only *appears* to rise in the east and set in the west because of Earth's motion. Our planet spins eastward like a top, and one full circle, called a rotation, takes 24 hours.

As Earth rotates, our view of the sky changes. During the day, we see the Sun. At night, we see stars and other planets because our location on Earth has spun away from where we can see the Sun.

To find out when the Sun will rise and set in your area, go to Almanac4kids.com/Sky.

The Long and Short of It

NORTH OF THE EQUATOR: On the first day of summer, around June 21, the North Pole tilts farthest toward the Sun. On this day, the local noon Sun appears at its highest point in the sky for the year, and we have the longest day length.

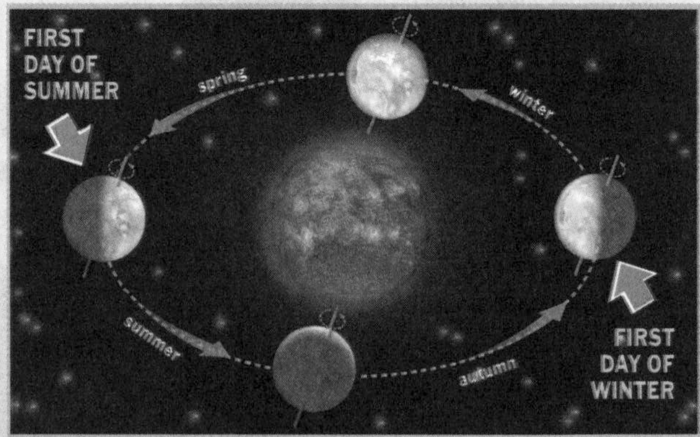

On the first day of winter, around December 21, the North Pole tilts farthest away from the Sun. On this day, the local noon Sun appears at its lowest point in the sky for the year, and we have the shortest day length.

SOUTH OF THE EQUATOR: The longest day occurs around December 21 and the shortest day is around June 21. This is because when the North Pole tilts toward the Sun, the South Pole tilts away, and when the South Pole tilts toward the Sun, the North Pole tilts away.

HOW LONG IS A DAY?

The total hours and minutes between the sunrise and sunset are the "day length," which can vary depending on how far north or south of the equator you are.

- **Day length at the equator is about 12 hours all year.**
- **Day length at the poles is extreme.** Once per year, the day length is 24 hours. Then it becomes progressively shorter, until there is no "day"—only night—for 24 hours. Then daylight returns, a little more each day.

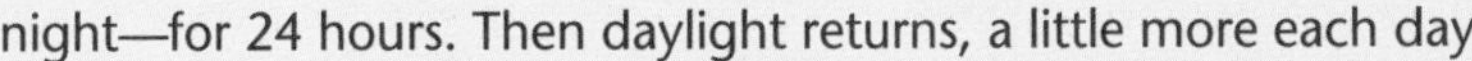

What Is Local Noon?

Noon on a clock occurs at the same moment throughout a time zone, such as Eastern or Mountain, which can be hundreds of miles wide. "Local noon," which can differ from clock noon by more than 60 minutes, occurs when the Sun "crosses" an imaginary line that runs from the North Pole directly over your head to the South Pole. When the Sun goes across that line, it is at its highest point in the sky for that day. It's exactly south if you're north of the equator and exactly north if you're south of the equator.

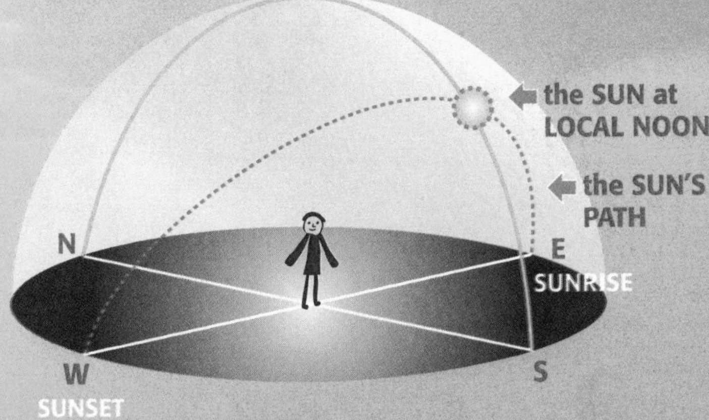

Got Your Head in the CLOUDS?

I saw two clouds at morning,
Tinged by the rising Sun,
And in the dawn
They floated on
And mingled into one.

–John G. C. Brainard,
American poet (1796–1828)

An understanding of cloud types helps in predicting the weather. Clouds are classified by their shape and by their height in the atmosphere.

Low Clouds

form below 6,500 feet and are primarily water droplets but may be ice or snow particles

Clouds floating low and casting shadows on the ground are usually followed by rain.

STRATUS clouds often appear as a dull-gray blanket on the sky. They sometimes produce drizzle or fine snow.

STRATOCUMULUS clouds, caused from the breakup of a large cumulus cloud, appear as broad, lumpy sheets. These usually indicate dry weather.

NIMBOSTRATUS clouds are similar to stratus clouds, but they are darker and have rougher bases. These bring rain or snow almost constantly for long periods.

Refreshing showers or heavy rains are near,
When piled in fleecy heaps the clouds appear.

Middle Clouds

form at 6,500 to 20,000 feet and are primarily water droplets but may be ice crystals

ALTOCUMULUS clouds usually appear as layers of puffy, round cloudlets. When these occur in the morning, expect afternoon thunderstorms.

ALTOSTRATUS clouds appear as gray sheets that cover all or most of the sky. They are so thick that they obscure the Sun; it appears as only a bright area in the sky. These often occur a few hours ahead of warm air that brings rain.

continued

Take a hint from these Latin root words:

- ***Cirro*** **or** ***cirrus*** **means curl (of hair)**
- ***Cumulus*** **means heap**
- ***Nimbus*** **means rain**
- ***Stratus*** **means spread or stretched**

High Clouds

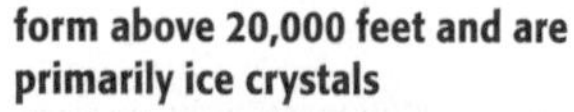

form above 20,000 feet and are primarily ice crystals

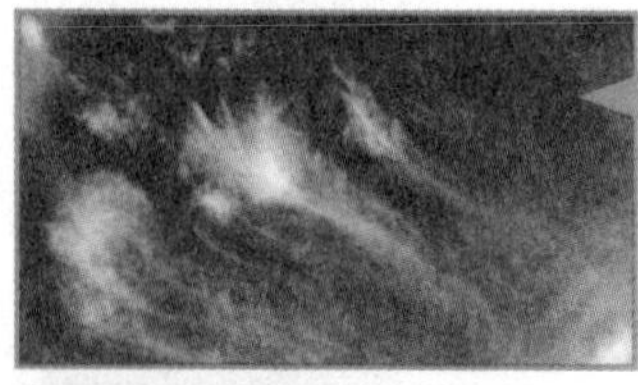

CIRRUS clouds are wispy and often spread across the sky. Streaming cirrus clouds are called "mares' tails." A gradual increase in these may signal a warm front on the way.

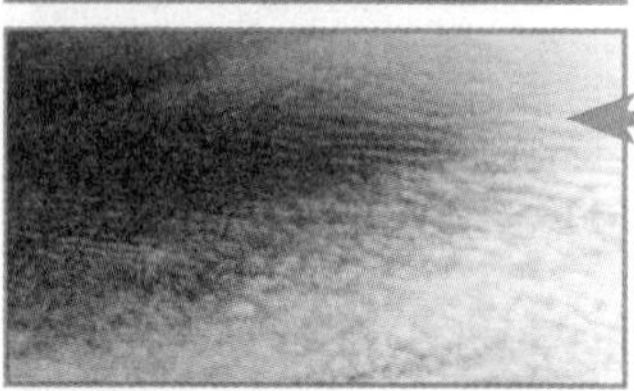

CIRROCUMULUS clouds are rippled or grainy. When they resemble diamond-shape fish scales, the effect is called a "mackerel sky." When these clouds begin to replace cirrus clouds, a storm may follow, as in the folk saying, "Mackerel sky, storm is nigh."

CIRROSTRATUS clouds spread in a thin sheet, giving the sky a whitish appearance. They indicate a change in the weather: if they thicken, it might rain; if they thin, expect fair conditions.

Vertically Developed Clouds

grow to heights in excess of 39,000 feet

CUMULUS clouds resemble white cotton balls. When they are scattered in the sky, they indicate fair, dry weather ahead. They can produce light, brief showers.

CUMULONIMBUS clouds are cumulus clouds that have grown high into the atmosphere. They have dark bases and, often, tops that resemble a blacksmith's anvil. These can produce heavy rain or snow, thunderstorms, and tornadoes.

LOOK . . . UP IN THE SKY . . .

It's a BIRD, it's a PLANE, it's . . .

NEPHELOCOCCYGIA!

Pronounced NEH-fih-lah-kock-SIH-jee-uh, this is the word for finding a shape—such as an animal, face, or other object—in a cloud. The term comes from the Greek words *nephelo*, meaning clouds, and *kokkyx*, meaning cuckoo. Aristophanes was the first to use the word, in his play *The Birds* in 414 B.C. Nephelococcygia was a "town" in the clouds built by birds, or a "cloud cuckoo land."

FROZEN

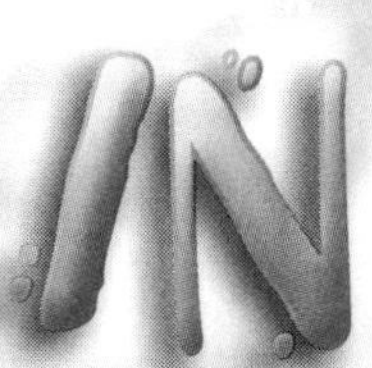

IN TIME

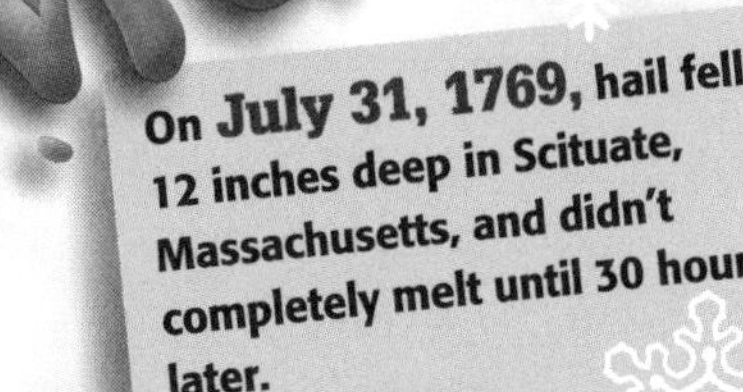

On July 31, 1769, hail fell 12 inches deep in Scituate, Massachusetts, and didn't completely melt until 30 hours later.

On **January 23, 1935,** in Iroquois Falls, Ontario, it was –73°F—so cold that the noise made by squeaking sleds scared horses.

In **January 1938,** in neighborhoods near Saskatoon, Saskatchewan, it was –51°F—so cold that kids could hear the school bus creaking 10 to 15 minutes before it arrived at their stop.

On February 19, 1959, a 7-day-long storm on Mt. Shasta, California, ended, leaving 189 inches of snow.

On **June 29, 1963,** the Livingston (Alberta) Ranger Station received 44 inches of snow—the largest summer snowfall ever recorded in Canada.

On December 19, 1983, in Moosomin, Saskatchewan, it was –43°F—so cold that several children got stuck to their playground equipment and had to be thawed off.

On **July 21, 1983,** in Vostok, Antarctica, it was –128.6°F, the world's coldest recorded temperature.

CONTINUED

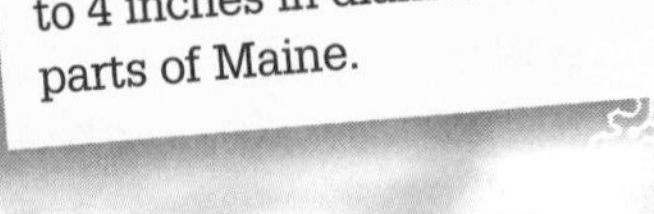

On **June 1, 1986,** hail up to 4 inches in diameter fell in parts of Maine.

On **January 15, 1994,** in Kapuskasing, Ontario, it was –45°F—so cold that tires fell off the rims of cars.

On September 23, 1989, in Richmond, Virginia, the temperature fell from 84°F to 54°F in 2 hours.

On **July 24, 1996,** hail the size of oranges fell on Calgary, Alberta.

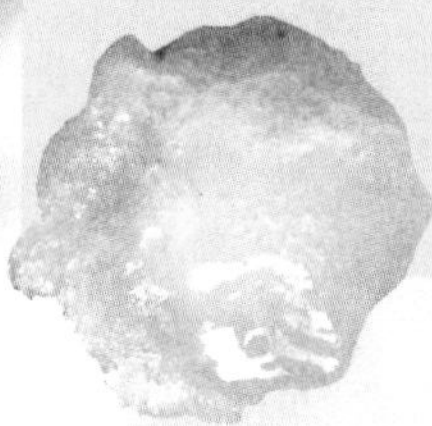

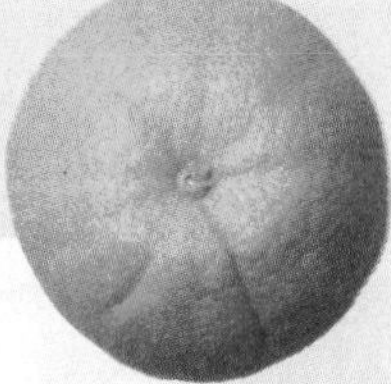

On February 29, 2008 (Leap Day!), the world's largest snowwoman (122 feet, 1 inch high) was dedicated in Bethel, Maine.

On **January 26 and 27, 2009,** sleet, snow, and freezing rain coated parts of Kentucky with an inch of ice, causing widespread power outages and canceling school for a week.

On **January 6, 2010,** temperatures in Miami, Florida, dropped to around 35°F—cold enough for iguanas to enter a hibernation state similar to sleep and fall out of trees.

On **July 23, 2010,** a hailstone weighing 1 pound 15 ounces and measuring 8 inches in diameter broke through a deck in Vivian, South Dakota, during a severe thunderstorm. Its weight and diameter were the largest ever recorded for a hailstone recovered in the United States.

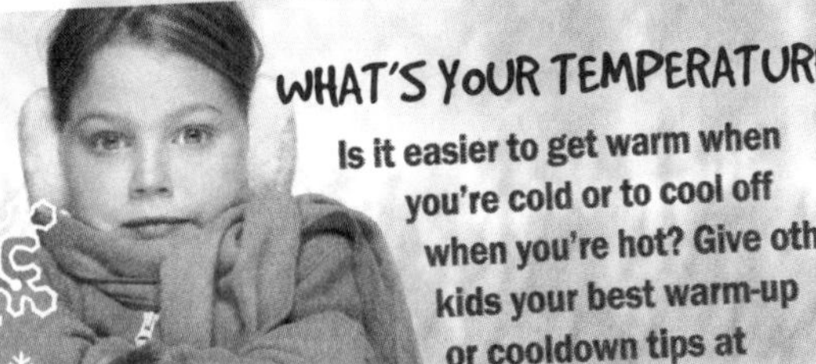

WHAT'S YOUR TEMPERATURE?

Is it easier to get warm when you're cold or to cool off when you're hot? Give other kids your best warm-up or cooldown tips at Almanac4kids.com/TellUs.

The Windchill Factor

As the wind speed increases, your body loses heat more rapidly, making the air feel colder than it really is. The combination of cold temperature and high wind creates such a severe cooling effect that your flesh can actually freeze! Check out this chart to see how cold you'll feel.

WIND SPEED (mph)	TEMPERATURE (°F)														
Calm	**35**	**30**	**25**	**20**	**15**	**10**	**5**	**0**	**–5**	**–10**	**–15**	**–20**	**–25**	**–30**	**–35**
5	31	25	19	13	7	1	–5	–11	–16	–22	–28	–34	–40	–46	–52
10	27	21	15	9	3	–4	–10	–16	–22	–28	–35	–41	–47	–53	–59
15	25	19	13	6	0	–7	–13	–19	–26	–32	–39	–45	–51	–58	–64
20	24	17	11	4	–2	–9	–15	–22	–29	–35	–42	–48	–55	–61	–68
25	23	16	9	3	–4	–11	–17	–24	–31	–37	–44	–51	–58	–64	–71
30	22	15	8	1	–5	–12	–19	–26	–33	–39	–46	–53	–60	–67	–73
35	21	14	7	0	–7	–14	–21	–27	–34	–41	–48	–55	–62	–69	–76
40	20	13	6	–1	–8	–15	–22	–29	–36	–43	–50	–57	–64	–71	–78
45	19	12	5	–2	–9	–16	–23	–30	–37	–44	–51	–58	–65	–72	–79
50	19	12	4	–3	–10	–17	–24	–31	–38	–45	–52	–60	–67	–74	–81
55	18	11	4	–3	–11	–18	–25	–32	–39	–46	–54	–61	–68	–75	–82
60	17	10	3	–4	–11	–19	–26	–33	–40	–48	–55	–62	–69	–76	–84

Frostbite occurs in **30 minutes** **10 minutes** **5 minutes**

To convert Fahrenheit to Celsius, use: °C = (°F – 32)/1.8

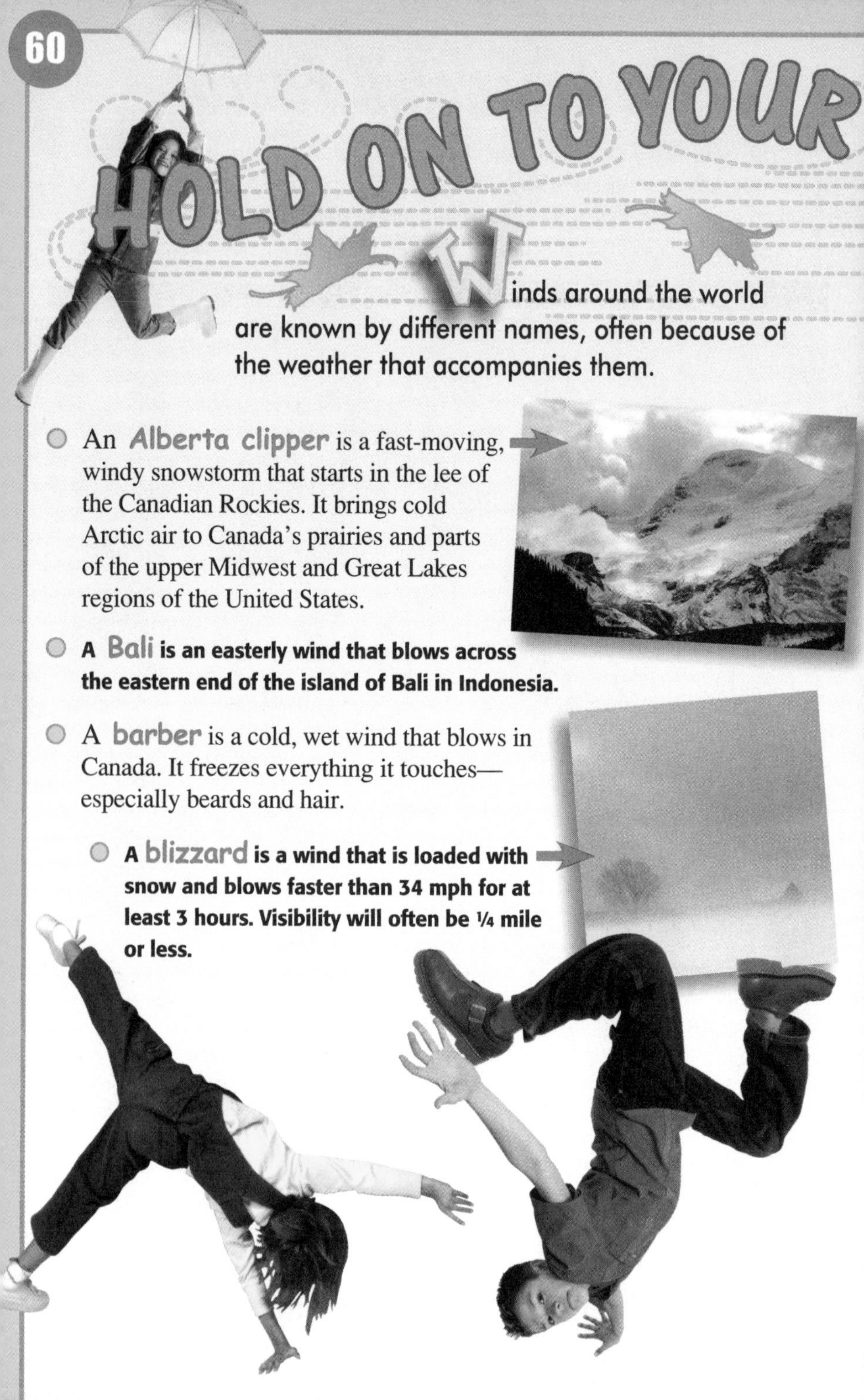

HOLD ON TO YOUR

Winds around the world are known by different names, often because of the weather that accompanies them.

- An **Alberta clipper** is a fast-moving, windy snowstorm that starts in the lee of the Canadian Rockies. It brings cold Arctic air to Canada's prairies and parts of the upper Midwest and Great Lakes regions of the United States.
- **A Bali is an easterly wind that blows across the eastern end of the island of Bali in Indonesia.**
- A **barber** is a cold, wet wind that blows in Canada. It freezes everything it touches—especially beards and hair.
- **A blizzard is a wind that is loaded with snow and blows faster than 34 mph for at least 3 hours. Visibility will often be ¼ mile or less.**

HA!

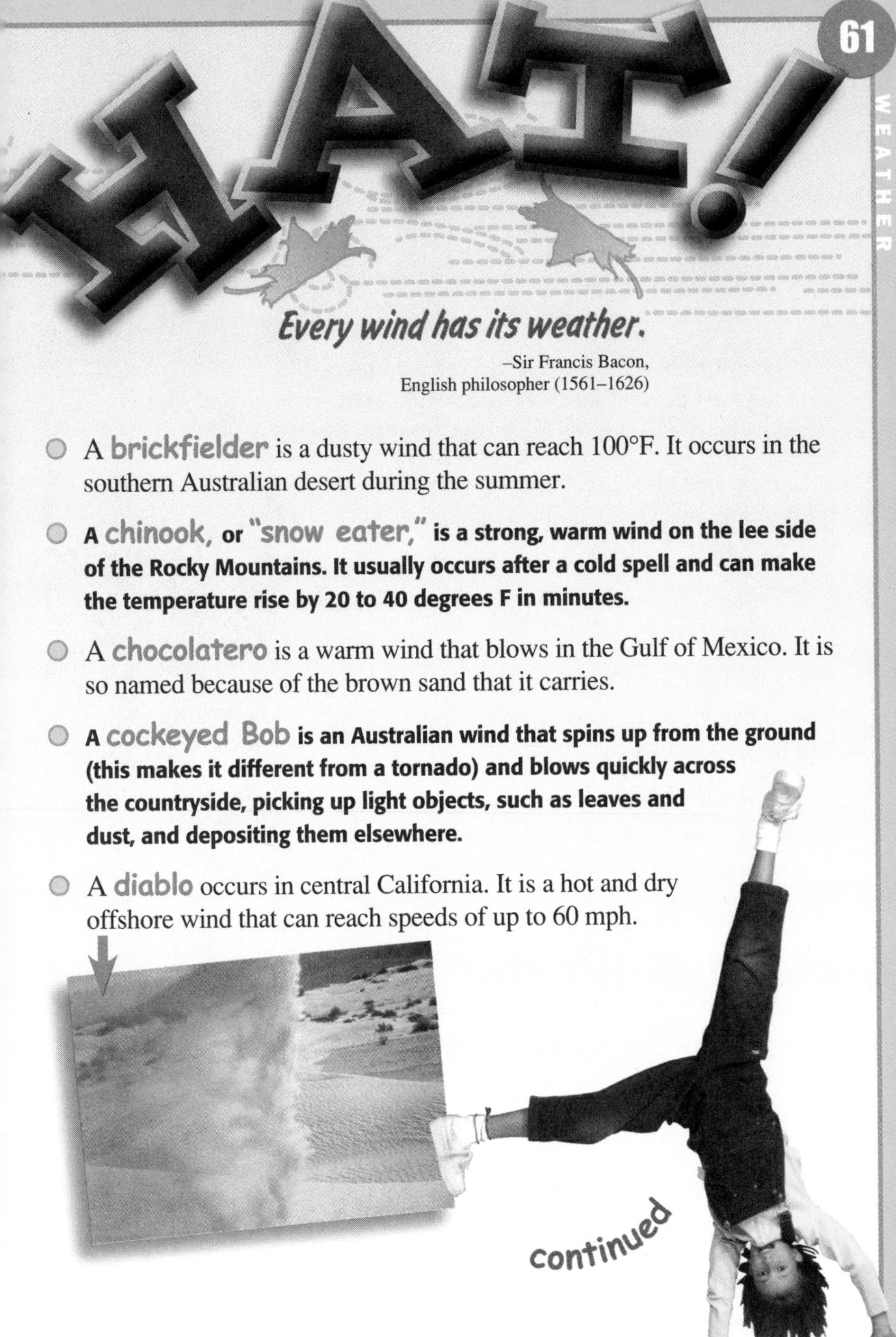

Every wind has its weather.

–Sir Francis Bacon,
English philosopher (1561–1626)

- A **brickfielder** is a dusty wind that can reach 100°F. It occurs in the southern Australian desert during the summer.
- **A chinook, or "snow eater," is a strong, warm wind on the lee side of the Rocky Mountains. It usually occurs after a cold spell and can make the temperature rise by 20 to 40 degrees F in minutes.**
- A **chocolatero** is a warm wind that blows in the Gulf of Mexico. It is so named because of the brown sand that it carries.
- **A cockeyed Bob is an Australian wind that spins up from the ground (this makes it different from a tornado) and blows quickly across the countryside, picking up light objects, such as leaves and dust, and depositing them elsewhere.**
- A **diablo** occurs in central California. It is a hot and dry offshore wind that can reach speeds of up to 60 mph.

- A **dust devil** is a whirlwind that develops from extreme surface heating. It is smaller than a tornado and rises from the ground, sometimes reaching 500 to 1,000 feet.
- An **elephanta** blows on India's Malabar coast from September to October and marks the end of the southwest monsoon.
- A **Fremantle doctor** is a cooling sea breeze on the west coast of Australia, near Perth, between noon and 3:00 P.M. almost every day. It is the most consistent wind in the world.
- **Lips** is what Greeks call a warm, dry wind caused by air moving down a mountain.
- A **maestro** is a cold and usually dry north wind on the western shore of the Adriatic Sea, especially in the summer.
- A **Santa Ana** is a strong, warm, dry, offshore wind that blows through southern California in late fall and winter.
- A **simoom** is a very hot and dry wind in African and Asian deserts during spring and summer. It lasts only 20 minutes but can reshape the desert landscape by moving a lot of sand.
- A **sirocco** is a hot, dry, dusty wind from the Sahara Desert. It can be about 110°F during the day and more than 86°F at night.
- A **sky sweeper** is a warm, dry wind blowing on the Spanish island of Majorca. It blows down mountains and speeds up, creating a rise in the temperature.
- A **southerly buster** is a sea breeze along the coast near Sydney, Australia, where its chilly air can be uncomfortable. Its cool wind is welcome farther inland on hot days.
- A **Squamish** is a strong and often violent wind that occurs in inlets in British Columbia. It can reach speeds of 20 mph offshore.
- A **zephyr** is a gentle breeze from the west on or near the summer solstice (the longest day of the year) in the Northern Hemisphere.

The WIND

I saw you toss the kites on high
And blow the birds about the sky;
And all around I heard you pass,
Like ladies' skirts across the grass—
O wind, a-blowing all day long,
O wind, that sings so loud a song!

I saw the different things you did,
But always you yourself you hid.
I felt you push, I heard you call,
I could not see yourself at all—
O wind, a-blowing all day long,
O wind, that sings so loud a song!

O you that are so strong and cold,
O blower, are you young or old?
Are you a beast of field and tree,
Or just a stronger child than me?
O wind, a-blowing all day long,
O wind, that sings so loud a song!

–Robert Louis Stevenson,
Scottish writer (1850–94)

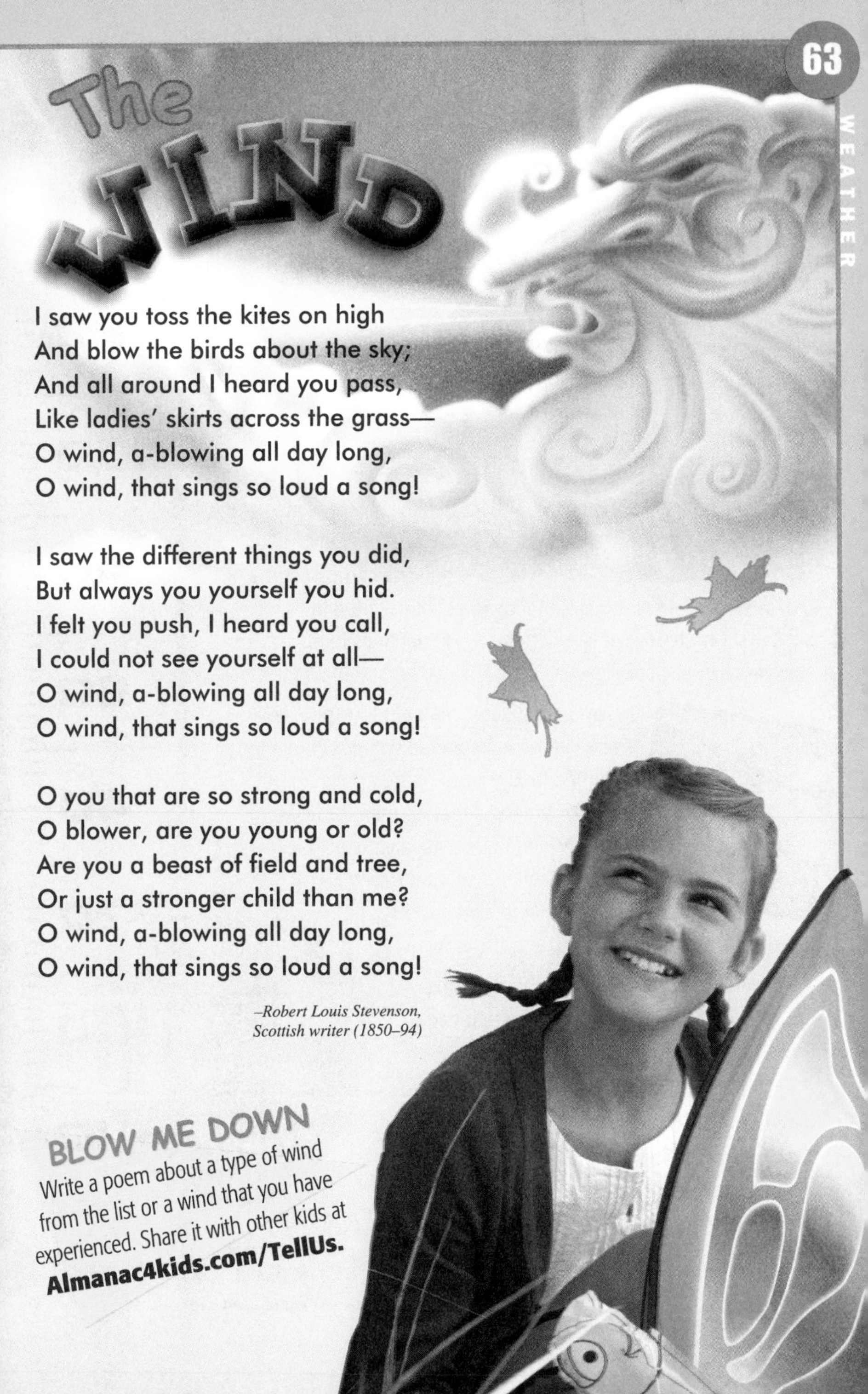

BLOW ME DOWN

Write a poem about a type of wind from the list or a wind that you have experienced. Share it with other kids at **Almanac4kids.com/TellUs.**

MEET the Thermometer Men

MR. FAHRENHEIT

Daniel Gabriel Fahrenheit was born on May 24, 1686, in Danzig, Germany (now Gdansk, Poland). When he was 15, both of his parents accidentally ate poisonous mushrooms and died. Daniel's guardians, hoping to get him started in business, sent him to Amsterdam in the Netherlands to be an apprentice to a shopkeeper.

This plan did not work out as expected. Daniel became fascinated with thermometry, the then-new science of measuring temperature and making thermometers. He decided to become a glassblower and scientific instrument maker. He lost interest in the shop, began misbehaving, and ran away.

Daniel traveled widely throughout Europe and studied his craft. Eventually, he returned to Amsterdam, where he built a successful business making glass instruments.

In those days, no two thermometers were alike, making it impossible to compare temperatures in different places. "Degrees" were unknown. People described the temperature simply as "hot" or "very hot," or "cold" or "very cold." Daniel was determined to develop a method for measuring temperature using a thermometer.

The birthplace of Daniel Fahrenheit

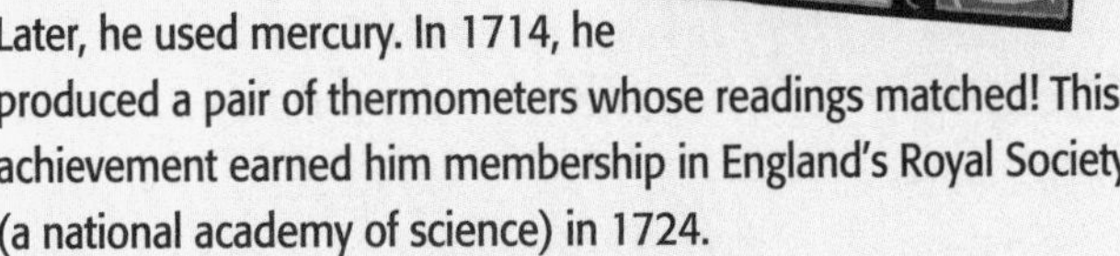

With no formal training in science, Daniel worked on this project for many years. In his early instruments, he used alcohol. Later, he used mercury. In 1714, he produced a pair of thermometers whose readings matched! This achievement earned him membership in England's Royal Society (a national academy of science) in 1724.

The Fahrenheit (F) scale sets 32 degrees as the freezing point of water and 212 degrees as the boiling point. (Daniel's "zero" degrees was the temperature reached by mixing equal weights of ice water and ammonium chloride, a type of salt.) Today, Fahrenheit is used mainly in the United States.

A Degree of Danger

Mercury, a liquid metal, is no longer considered safe to use in thermometers. It can evaporate easily, giving off toxic chemicals. Exposure to mercury can cause health problems for humans and animals and harm our environment.

MR. CELSIUS

Anders Celsius

Anders Celsius was born on November 27, 1701, in Uppsala, Sweden. Like his father and grandfather, Anders loved studying the night sky and eventually became an astronomer. He followed in his father's footsteps and taught astronomy at the local university. Anders was fascinated by the aurora borealis, or northern lights. He was the first to see a relationship between these lights and Earth's magnetic field.

CONTINUED

Anders's studies enabled him to visit most of Europe's major observatories. During a trip to Lapland in northern Sweden, he measured a degree of longitude, which helped to confirm the shape of Earth. This led Anders to establish the Celsius Observatory in 1741. There, he made some of the first measurements of the brightness, or magnitude, of stars by using a device other than the human eye.

Anders is most famous for the invention in 1742 of a 100-point temperature scale that has the freezing and boiling points of water at its extremes. (Anders's first scale measured freezing as 100 degrees and boiling as 0 degrees. After his death in 1744, these were reversed.) Anders described his scale as "centigrade" (Latin for "one hundred steps"). In 1948, Anders's invention became commonly known as the Celsius scale. Scientists often use the Celsius scale for their work.

COMPARE THE SCALES

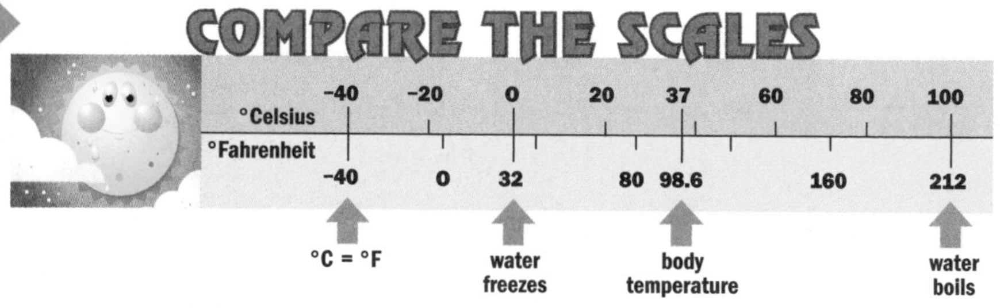

COUNT CRICKET CHIRPS!

When you don't have a thermometer handy, you can tell the temperature by listening to a cricket. For the temperature in degrees . . .

FAHRENHEIT: Count the chirps in 14 seconds and add 37.

CELSIUS: Count the chirps in 25 seconds, divide by 3, and add 4.

HINT: Crickets chirp faster when it's warm and more slowly when it's cool.

ACCORDING TO FOLKLORE AND FARMERS, THE NATURAL WORLD MAY HOLD SOME UNSCIENTIFIC YET SENSIBLE CLUES TO NEXT WINTER'S WEATHER

PERSIMMON

Use a ripe, homegrown persimmon if possible. Store-bought ones are often seedless—and you need the seed!

Cut the persimmon in half and remove the seed. Cut the seed open and look at the shape of the kernel inside. If the kernel is shaped like . . .

- A SPOON, THINK SHOVEL: **Expect lots of heavy, wet snow.**

- A FORK, THINK EMPTY SHOVEL: **Expect powdery, light snow and a mild winter.**
- A KNIFE, THINK SHARP: **Expect icy surfaces, cutting winds, and stormy conditions.**

CONTINUED

GOOSE BREASTBONE

As some families did in years past around Thanksgiving, you can use the breastbone from a roast goose to predict the weather. Carefully remove it from the carcass, clean it, and put it on the shelf to dry. If the breastbone turns . . .

- **white, a mild winter lies ahead.**
- **purple at the two ends, a cold spring can be expected.**
- **blue, in streaks, clear weather will last until New Year's Day.**
- **blue, black, or purple all over, begin preparations for a bad winter. The darker the color, the tougher the winter ahead will be.**

PIG SPLEEN

Some farmers swear by this technique. Only the spleens of freshly slaughtered pigs are used. Here's how it works: The spleen is divided visually (without cutting) into six portions. Each area represents 1 month. The top portion of the spleen (closest to the pig's head) represents the current month. The bottom indicates the end of the upcoming 6-month period.

- **Where the spleen thickens, a change in the weather is indicated, usually pointing to a cold spell.**
- **Where the spleen has a significant bulge, expect even more inclement weather.**

WOOLLY BEAR

In the fall, look for this black-and-brown fuzzy caterpillar, also known as a woolly worm, on the sidewalk, in the garden, or in the woods under a tree limb. If the brown bristles in the middle of its body are . . .

- **wide, the winter will be mild.**
- **narrow, the winter will be cold.**

EXPERTS IN THE FIELD

When a cow tries to scratch its ear,
It means a shower is very near;
When it thumps its ribs with its tail,
Look out for thunder, lightning,
hail.

When pigs carry sticks,
The clouds will play tricks;
When they lie in the mud,
No fears of a flood.

The goose and the gander
Begin to meander;
The matter is plain:
They are dancing for rain.

Creatures That GLOW

Some insects, fish, mollusks, fungi, and worms produce a glow called bioluminescence, or "living light." The glow comes from internal chemical reactions You can find these organisms if you look carefully . .

In the AIR

FIREFLIES, also called lightning bugs, are actuall nocturnal beetles They exist on every continent excep Antarctica. More than 170 species cal North America home, but, for some unknown reason they are seldom found west o Kansas. The best area in North America for viewing fireflies is along the Florida–Georgia border, from the

Big Bend coast to the Okefenokee Swamp.

Fireflies light up to send a mating call. The males flash as they fly, while the females stay on the ground or on low bushes, flashing back. (Females seldom fly.) Their adulthood lasts for only a few weeks, and they spend every night courting. Most don't even eat! The larvae, or babies, of most firefly species also glow. They're called GLOWWORMS.

Above, a close-up view of a firefly

Below, blue glowworms light up the Waitomo Glowworm Caves in New Zealand.

- A fireflyer is someone with a passion for fireflies.
- One of the most popular folk songs in Japan is "The Light of the Firefly," set to the music of "Auld Lang Syne."

FLASH for Fireflies

To attract fireflies, find one, count the number of its flashes, their duration, and the time between flashes. Then mimic the flash pattern with a small flashlight.

CONTIN

At SEA

More than 90 percent of deep-sea animals are thought to be BIOLUMINESCENT. Organisms such as comb jellies, lantern or flashlight fish, certain squid and ocean worms, and a swimming sea cucumber use bioluminescence to see, lure, or scare away other creatures.

The glowing sea creatures that are easiest to spot are microscopic organisms called DINOFLAGELLATES. They light up if they are moved, such as by waves, wind, fish, and boats. When these organisms wash up on the beach and you step on them, you leave "glowing" footprints in the sand.

Transparent, hula-skirt siphonophores like this one can be found in both the Arctic and Pacific oceans.

► Strangely, a mysterious, glowing, milky-color part of the Indian Ocean has been noted only twice, *both times on January 27 . . .*

- by a satellite, which captured images of the phenomenon in 1995.
- by the submarine *Nautilus* in Jules Verne's novel *20,000 Leagues Under the Sea*—published in 1870.

Above, a column of glowing kelp

Right, photophores light up a squid's eyes.

On the GROUND

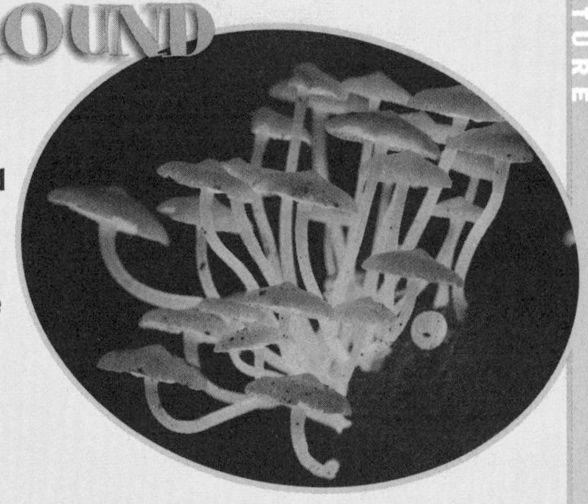

Explore the woods at night and look for an eerie, blue-green glow. Here, we call it FOXFIRE and TOUCHWOOD, while Irish and Scottish folktales refer to it as fairy fire and will-o'-the-wisp. The light comes from several species of fungi found on the ground; in moist, decaying logs; and on tree stumps. There are more than 40 species of luminescent fungi. Most glow green, white, yellow, or blue. Scientists aren't sure why.

A common fungus found in North America, Europe, and Asia is the HONEY MUSHROOM. The glow of its rootlike parts looks like a stain on wood and lasts for up to 8 weeks.

Above, fluorescent fungus glows at night in Borneo, Malaysia.

Below, a honey mushroom fungus grows in North America.

- Ben Franklin suggested that foxfire be used to light the instrument panel of the world's first submarine, built in 1775 and used during a secret mission against the British in the Revolutionary War. Ben's idea was declined.
- In Mark Twain's novel *The Adventures of Tom Sawyer,* Tom and Huck Finn use foxfire for light when digging a tunnel to free Jim.

Get to Know a GRASS

Grasshoppers can be found almost anywhere—caves, deserts, meadows, mountains, and wetlands. The more than 10,000 known species bouncing across the globe can be divided into two major types, **long-horned** (shown above) and **short-horned.**

The "horn" refers to the antennae. A long-horned

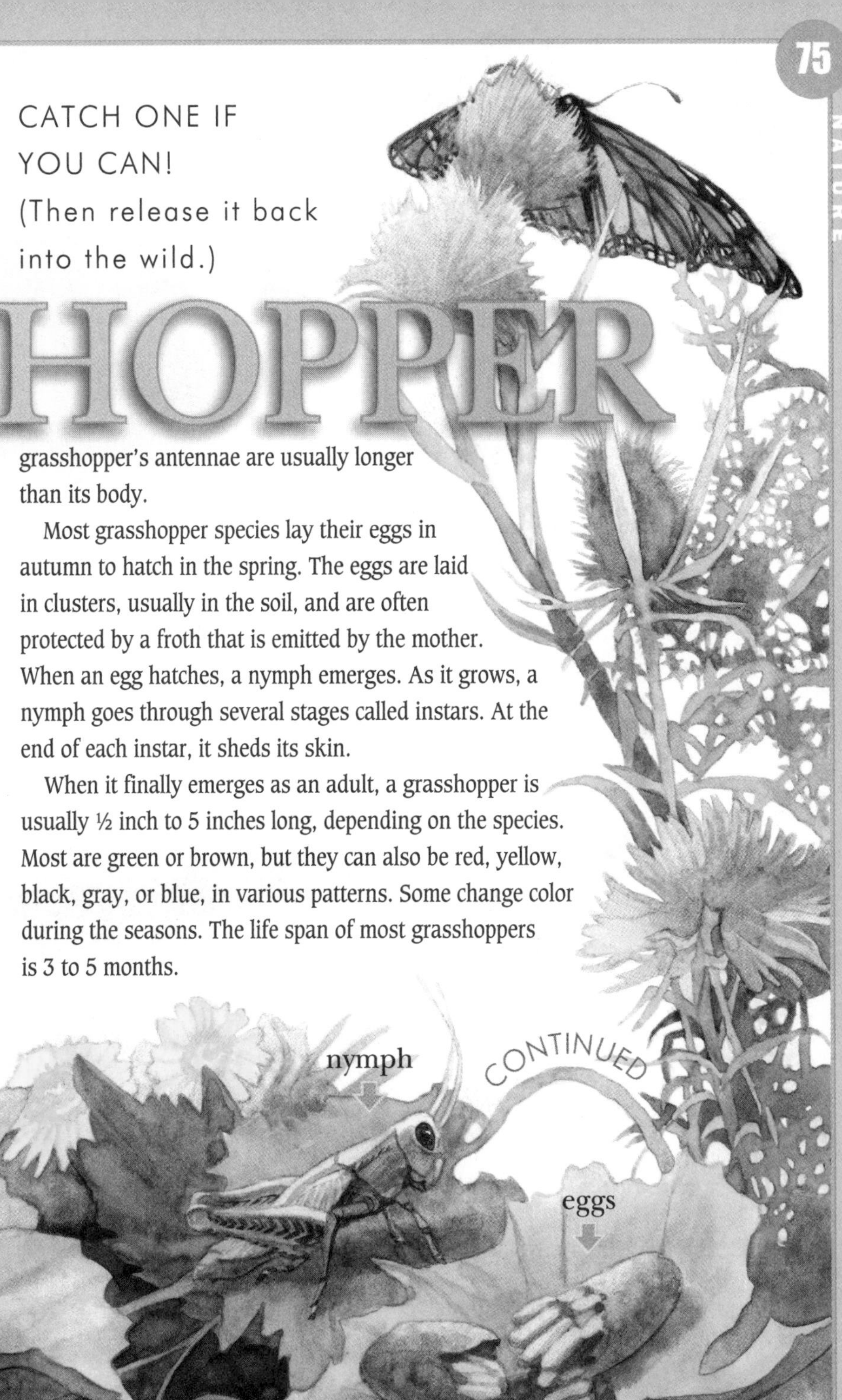

CATCH ONE IF YOU CAN! (Then release it back into the wild.)

HOPPER

grasshopper's antennae are usually longer than its body.

Most grasshopper species lay their eggs in autumn to hatch in the spring. The eggs are laid in clusters, usually in the soil, and are often protected by a froth that is emitted by the mother. When an egg hatches, a nymph emerges. As it grows, a nymph goes through several stages called instars. At the end of each instar, it sheds its skin.

When it finally emerges as an adult, a grasshopper is usually ½ inch to 5 inches long, depending on the species. Most are green or brown, but they can also be red, yellow, black, gray, or blue, in various patterns. Some change color during the seasons. The life span of most grasshoppers is 3 to 5 months.

CONTINUED

A GRASSHOPPER HAS . . .

THREE MAIN BODY PARTS:

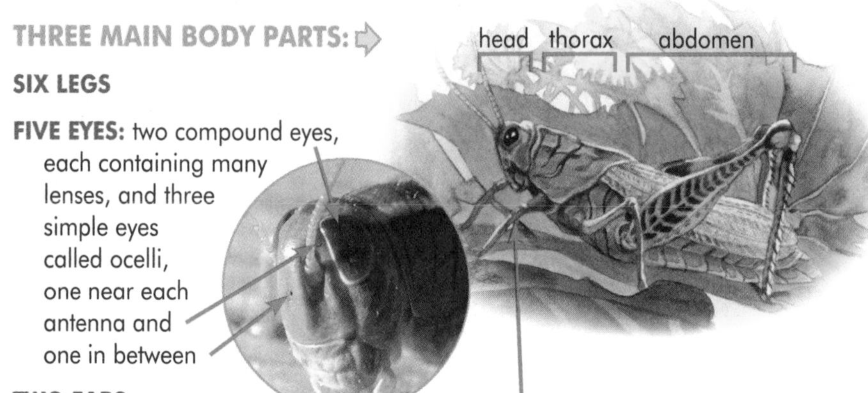

SIX LEGS

FIVE EYES: two compound eyes, each containing many lenses, and three simple eyes called ocelli, one near each antenna and one in between

TWO EARS:
A long-horned grasshopper's ears are on its front legs; a short-horned grasshopper has an ear on each side of its abdomen.

WINGS: two pairs, in most cases. A few flightless species have short, stubby wings or none at all. Hard forewings protect the fragile hind wings while folded. Many grasshoppers rub or clap their wings together or against other body parts, such as their legs, to make sounds.

Grasshoppers, depending on the species, eat grasses, grains, or other vegetation, including weeds or plants that are poisonous to cattle. A few eat other insects. Occasionally, hoppers eat paint, caulking, or the mesh in a window screen.

IT SPITS!

To protect themselves from predators such as birds, rodents, and other insects, some grasshoppers spit a brown liquid nicknamed "tobacco juice" that startles the attacker and gives the hopper time to escape.

Others scare away predators by exposing bright colors on their hind wings or sides or hide by mimicking bark or dead leaves. Some species store toxic chemicals that make them taste awful.

Saved by St. Urho?

MANY PEOPLE, especially those of Finnish descent, celebrate March 16 as St. Urho's Day. Legend has it that Urho drove grasshoppers out of the vineyards of ancient Finland. Festivities include parades and potluck meals, and celebrants wear purple and green, despite the fact that 32 species of grasshopper continue to thrive in Finland.

What goes into Grasshopper Pie?

NOT INSECTS! Mint, marshmallow, and whipped cream. Learn how to make one at Almanac4kids.com /GrasshopperPie.

Do You Know Any . . .

KOOKY Katydids?

Some scientists classify **KATYDIDS** as a type of long-horned grasshopper. Most of the approximately 6,000 species live in the tropics. They are named after one species that repeatedly calls out "Katy did, Katy didn't" each evening. They could have been named "copy Katys" for their ability to blend in with leaves or twigs and mimic other insects, such as moths or wasps.

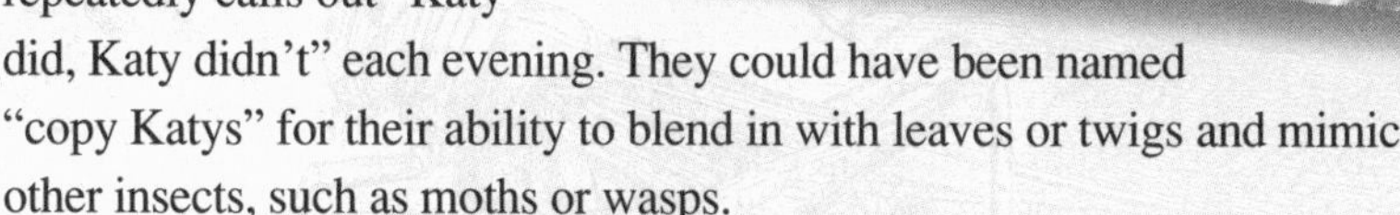

When katydids begin to sing, it's said that there are only 6 more weeks of summer.

CONTINUED

LOCO LOCUSTS?

LOCUSTS like to be alone, but with the right combination of rain, vegetation, and timing, these short-horned grasshoppers will breed in high numbers, forming a plague, or swarm.

Kansas was nicknamed the Grasshopper State after a plague of Rocky Mountain locusts attacked the area in 1874. The Kansas State Historical Society reports that during this time, the insects ate the wool off sheep, the clothing off people, and the wooden handles off tools.

Scientists use satellites to monitor weather patterns and plants to help predict locust outbreaks, especially those of the destructive desert locust in Africa and Asia.

COMEBACK Cicadas?

CICADAS, often mistaken for locusts, are not grasshoppers. Some cicadas are periodical: They tend to mature together. For example, once every 17 years, thousands of cicada nymphs of a certain brood emerge from the ground and climb trees and shrubs to molt into adults. Sometimes the shed skin of a cicada nymph can be found clinging to a tree trunk.

Dog-day cicadas emerge annually. Males sing during the Dog Days of summer (July 3 to August 11), which, according to folklore, are the hottest and most unhealthy days of the year (see article, p. 35). It is said that dry weather will follow their first song and frost will occur 6 weeks later.

WHY (AND HOW) Leaves Change Color

It happens every year. Leaves change from glorious green to amazing yellows, oranges, and reds. Some people believe that cold weather makes leaves turn color, but sunlight starts and ends the process.

Leaves get their color from three pigments:

- **CHLOROPHYLL: green pigments**
- **CAROTENOIDS: yellow, orange, or gold pigments**
- **ANTHOCYANINS: red, blue, or purple pigments**

The Formula FOR FOLIAGE

Leaves have veins that carry fluid through them. To see the veins, hold a leaf up to a light.

During the long days and intense sunshine of spring and summer, chlorophylls in leaves give them their green color and help them to use sunlight to convert water and carbon dioxide into sugar. (This is called photosynthesis.) The sugar travels through the leaves' veins into the tree.

In autumn, as sunlight decreases and days get shorter, leaves make less and less sugar. Eventually, the chlorophylls decrease and the green color in the leaves begins to fade. Photosynthesis finally stops, and the veins at the bases of the leaf stems sometimes close, trapping sugars and causing the production of anthocyanins.

As this is happening, the yellow, orange, and gold carotenoids are revealed. The leaves aren't really "changing" color—these pigments are already there! They become visible when the chlorophylls are gone.

continued

Anthocyanins, which help a tree to use any remaining nutrients, may also appear. These combine with carotenoids to produce brilliant orange and red leaves.

Once the base of a leaf's stem is completely clogged, the leaf dies and is ready to fall. The wind then "pushes" the weakened leaf off the tree.

Fall's Well That Ends Well

Trees that lose their leaves are "deciduous," which comes from the Latin for "to fall off." You can identify trees by the color of their leaves in autumn:

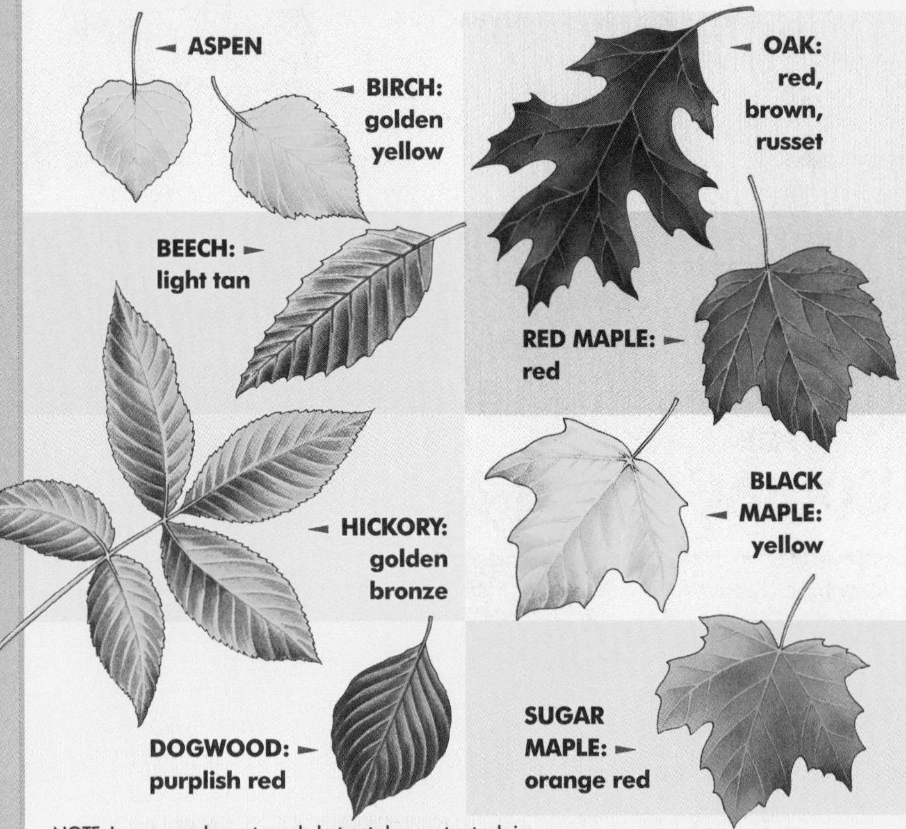

NOTE: Leaves are drawn to scale but not shown at actual size.

Not all deciduous trees produce leaves that turn spectacular colors. Some leaves just turn brown, shrivel up, and fall off. Once leaves hit the ground, bacteria, fungi, and earthworms break them down. As leaves decompose, they fill the soil with nutrients for plants and trees. Leaf layers also help to protect plant roots and absorb rainfall.

What's Weather Got to Do With It?

Leaves produce anthocyanin pigments on warm, sunny autumn days and during cool—not freezing!—nights. Carotenoids are already in the leaves; weather doesn't affect them.

The BEST weather conditions for BEAUTIFUL leaves of all colors are . . .

- a warm, wet spring
- a not-too-hot, not-too-dry summer
- warm, sunny days and cool nights in fall

The weather conditions that cause POOR fall foliage include . . .

- a hot, dry summer; green leaves may drop before their yellow, orange, and red colors are revealed
- heat and rain in autumn, which can result in dull colors
- a hard frost, which can kill the leaves before they begin to change

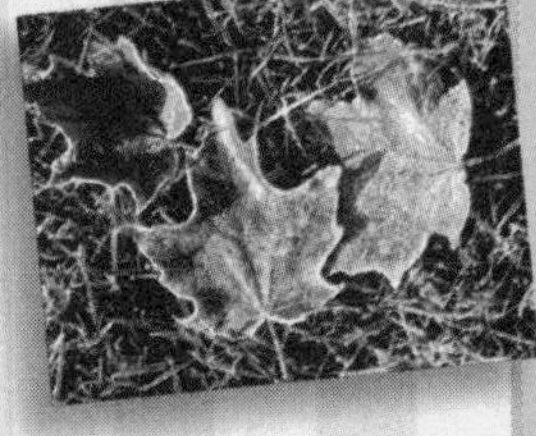

All the Time

ALL GREEN

Trees that do not lose leaves are called "evergreens." (They are "forever green"—get it?) These include pine, fir, and spruce trees. Evergreen trees . . .

- **have needles or leaves that do not change color and do not fall off every year.**
- **are hardy, which means that they do not freeze in winter. (There are also other evergreens that have adapted to grow in warm climates.)**

RED RITUALS

- In Japan, people enjoy *momiji oroshi* ("grated maple leaves"), a grated radish and red chile pepper sauce, and decorate dishes with maple leaves.
- To match the autumn leaves, some Japanese paint the woodwork on bridges and buildings red.

BE A Bird Brainiac!

SURPRISING FACTS about birds and MORE

In years past, people might say "Don't be a birdbrain!" to someone who was being silly. This was because scientists believed that birds' brains were primitive and that birds acted on instinct.

Now, neuroscientists have discovered that certain birds, such as parrots, have brains that enable them to learn and teach new sounds. Only humans, bats, dolphins, whales, elephants, and some birds have brains that can support these skills.

So, bird brainiacs, fly high with these facts.

ruby-throated hummingbird

bee-eater

parrots

black-crowned cranes

barn owl

Copycat Bird

Mockingbirds sing—but not their own song. They copy, or mock, the songs of other birds. Each imitation is repeated two or three times, and then it's on to another tune. A mockingbird may know 30 to 200 sounds, including other birdsongs, insect and amphibian sounds, and even the sounds of barking dogs, pianos, sirens, or squeaky gates. Often, mockingbirds are such good imitators that electronic analysis can't tell the imitation from the original.

CONTINUED

lilac-breasted roller

hoopoe

BEYOND FLOCKS

Group names for things are called **collective nouns.** Here are a few for specific birds:

- **charm of hummingbirds**
- **chattering of chicks**
- **colony of gulls**
- **congress of crows**
- **exaltation of larks**
- **gulp of cormorants**
- **mob of emus**
- **parliament of owls**
- **stand of flamingos**
- **unkindness of ravens**
- **watch of nightingales**

PASSENGER PIGEON PASSINGS

John James Audubon once saw a migration of passenger pigeons so big that it took 3 days to fly over his head. Such flocks would darken the sky, and their colonies, called "pigeon cities," were huge. In 1871, the largest colony ever described covered about two-thirds of the state of Wisconsin.

Over the years, massive hunting and forest-clearing led to the passenger pigeons' extinction. The last known one, **Martha,** named after Martha Washington, died in 1914 in the Cincinnati Zoo.

QUIRKY KIWI

New Zealand's national bird, the **kiwi,** is different from most birds:

- **Its feathers look like hair.**
- **It is the only bird that has nostrils at the end of its beak.**
- **It hatches from an enormous egg and is born fully feathered and able to live for a time on a large reserve of yolk in its belly.**

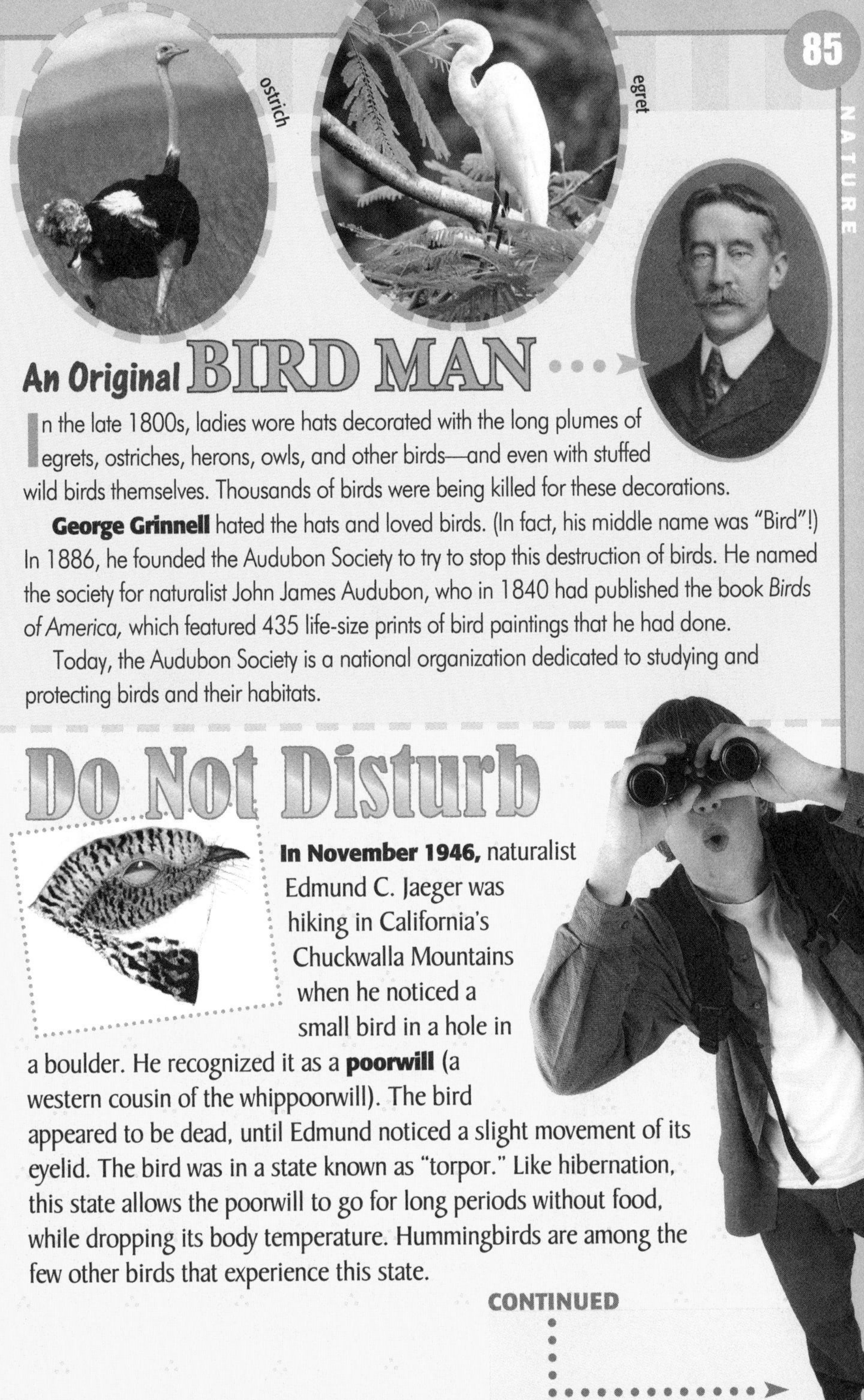

An Original BIRD MAN

In the late 1800s, ladies wore hats decorated with the long plumes of egrets, ostriches, herons, owls, and other birds—and even with stuffed wild birds themselves. Thousands of birds were being killed for these decorations.

George Grinnell hated the hats and loved birds. (In fact, his middle name was "Bird"!) In 1886, he founded the Audubon Society to try to stop this destruction of birds. He named the society for naturalist John James Audubon, who in 1840 had published the book *Birds of America,* which featured 435 life-size prints of bird paintings that he had done.

Today, the Audubon Society is a national organization dedicated to studying and protecting birds and their habitats.

Do Not Disturb

In November 1946, naturalist Edmund C. Jaeger was hiking in California's Chuckwalla Mountains when he noticed a small bird in a hole in a boulder. He recognized it as a **poorwill** (a western cousin of the whippoorwill). The bird appeared to be dead, until Edmund noticed a slight movement of its eyelid. The bird was in a state known as "torpor." Like hibernation, this state allows the poorwill to go for long periods without food, while dropping its body temperature. Hummingbirds are among the few other birds that experience this state.

CONTINUED

scarlet ibis

cape white-eye

DID YOU KNOW?

Largest bird eggs: ostrich eggs, which weigh about 3 pounds and are the size of a small football

Biggest bird egg ever: the 27-pound egg of the now extinct, 10-foot-tall, flightless elephant bird of Madagascar

Smallest bird eggs: hummingbird eggs, about the size of a pea or small jelly bean

NEAT NESTS

- **Osprey nests** are made of anything they can find—even bottles, fishnets, old rubber boots, and tin cans.
- **Bald eagles** enlarge their nests annually. The largest on record was 9½ feet wide and weighed over 2 tons!
- Made from spider silk and thistledown, **hummingbird nests** are about 1½ inches wide.
- **Cave swiftlets** of Southeast Asia build nests entirely out of their own saliva, which hardens when exposed to air. People collect saliva nests and sell them to restaurants, which clean them and use them for "bird's-nest soup," an expensive delicacy. (Some restaurants use noodles shaped like a bird's nest instead.)

HELP BIRDS BUILD NESTS!

barn swallows

black-shouldered kite

Put some of these things outside:

- yarn or string cut into 4- to 8-inch pieces
- human hair or horsehair, 4 to 6 inches long
- pet fur (that hasn't had flea or tick treatments)
- sheep's wool
- strips of cloth, about 1 inch wide by 6 inches long

If you find a nest, make sure that it's abandoned and then take a closer look. Use tweezers to "dissect" it.

Phoebe Snetsinger of Missouri started birdwatching in 1965 and eventually set a world record by spotting about 8,400 bird species in her lifetime. She died on a birding trip to Madagasar in 1999, shortly after sighting a rare bird called a **helmet vanga.**

Why do seagulls live by the sea?

Because if they lived by the bay, they'd be BAGELS.

THE ICKY ITCH PLANT

Leaves of three, let them be! *–old saying*

Poison ivy is as menacing as it sounds. If you touch it, you may get a nasty, itchy rash. The plant is a master of disguise, appearing just about anywhere:
- woods
- hiking trails
- roadsides
- fields
- beaches
- backyards

Fortunately, poison ivy can be easy to recognize: Its "leaf" is really three leaflets, each 2 to 4 inches long. Their edges may be smooth or have jagged points called teeth. Many leaflets have a notch on the sides and most end in a point. A plant can grow as . . .

- **ground cover,** 6 to 18 inches tall
- **a thick vine,** up to 30 feet long, with hairs, or aerial roots, on the stem
- **a shrub,** up to 10 feet tall

Young poison ivy leaves are reddish. Older ones are green. In the fall, the leaves can turn red, orange, or yellow.

In late spring and early summer, the plant produces tiny flowers. Berries appear in summer and early fall, at first green but then turning creamy white.

A typical poison ivy ground vine.

Near salt water, poison ivy leaves may appear waxy and curled.

The Poison Part

The leaves, stems, flowers, berries, and roots contain an oil called urushiol (yuh-ROO-shee-all). This is what causes the itchy rash. If you brush a plant, even gently, and bruise it, any oil present will be transferred to your skin or clothing.

Poison ivy leaves as they appear in the spring (above) and in the fall (below).

DID YOU KNOW?

Poison oak and poison sumac are in the same family as poison ivy. They all contain urushiol.

• • •

Many wild animals are not affected by poison ivy. Deer and small mammals eat the leaves, twigs, and berries. Birds love the berries, too.

• • •

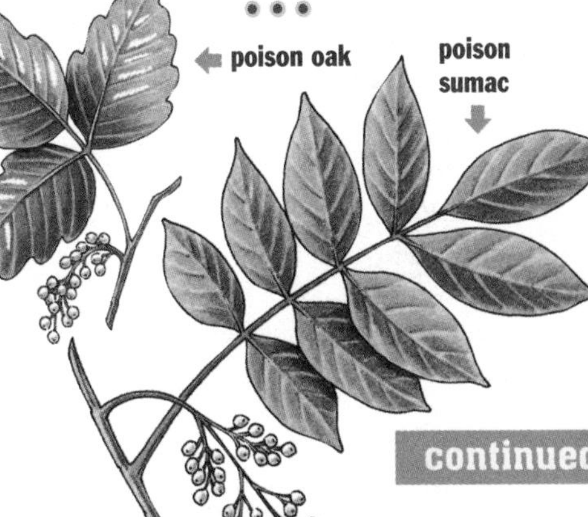

continued

WHEN you come in contact with poison ivy, you have 10 to 15 minutes before the oil will be absorbed into your skin.

- **Do not touch any body part,** especially your face.
- **Wash the exposed skin,** even under your fingernails, with soap and cool water.
- Separately from other laundry, **wash your clothing.** Also clean your shoes and any other items that may have been in contact with the oil, which can stay on your clothes for days—even years!

IF a red, bumpy, blistery, tingly rash develops within a few hours or days of contact, you've probably got poison ivy. In most cases, the rash heals within 2 weeks. Medicines, such as calamine lotion, can help to reduce the itch and help the healing. If necessary, see a doctor.

- **Keep cool;** heat increases the itch. Apply an ice pack to your skin—and try not to scratch!
- Even though scratching a blister will not spread the rash, **it's still best not to do it.** An infection could develop.

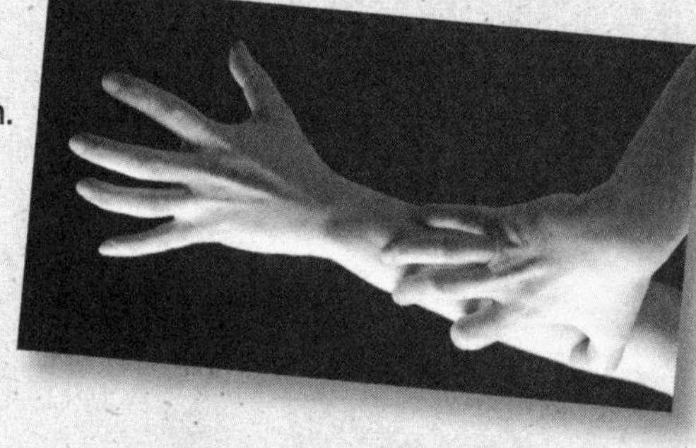

DON'T worry. No one can "catch" poison ivy by touching a rash.

NEVER burn poison ivy—and be sure to avoid mowed areas or burning brush piles that may contain the plant. Urushiol can become airborne, and you should not breathe it in.

Mother Nature's SECRET SERUM

Jewelweed is a 3- to 5-foot-tall plant with orange, spotted, trumpetlike flowers that often grows near poison ivy. If you touch poison ivy and can not wash up, crush a jewelweed stem and rub the juice on your skin. The sap is said to reduce symptoms. Then wash up as soon as you can!

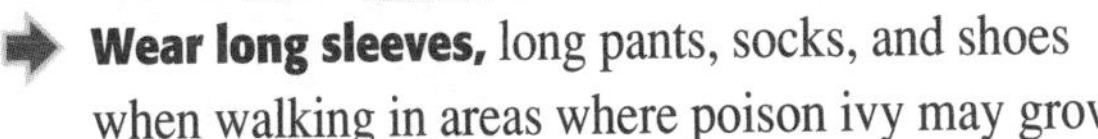

BE PREPARED

- **Wear long sleeves,** long pants, socks, and shoes when walking in areas where poison ivy may grow.
- **Wear nonabsorbent, heavy rubber gloves,** not cotton, when working where poison ivy may grow. (Wash the gloves afterward.)
- **Buy and apply special lotion** to help to block urushiol from being absorbed into your skin before going outdoors.
- **Keep pets and people safe!** Dogs, cats, and other furry animals that come in contact with poison ivy may not get a rash. But a pet can carry the oil on its fur and pass it on when petted.

You Say "TO-MAY-TO,"

Others call it *xitomatl*, "love apple,"

Centuries ago, tomatoes grew wild in the Andes mountains of Peru. Native Aztec people ate them raw and cooked, and named them *xitomatl* (zee-toe-MAH-tel), meaning "plump thing with a navel." Somehow, perhaps because birds carried away some seeds, the plants began growing in Central America and Mexico.

In 1519, Spanish explorer Hernan Cortés conquered Mexico and found these luscious red fruit. He brought plants back to Spain, where they produced abundant harvests. Other explorers took tomato plants to Asia, where they were an instant success.

Everyone loved tomatoes – until 1597.

That year, John Gerarde, an English barber-surgeon, wrote a book in which he declared tomatoes to be poisonous. Once enjoyed so much that it it was called the "love apple," the tomato suddenly became known as the "wolf peach." Word spread that tomatoes would cause frothing at the mouth, brain fever, and death, and people in Britain and North America stopped eating them.

Fear of tomatoes lasted for almost 200 years.

In the late 1700s, colonists in Georgia, Florida, and the Carolinas began growing and eating tomatoes. Pioneers and settlers moving to new territories brought seeds and plants with them. Soon tomatoes were growing and being eaten in widespread areas.

I Say "TO-MAH-TO"

or simply delicious.

A world without tomatoes is like a string quartet without violins.

–Laurie Colwin, American writer (1944–92)

CONTINUED

Still, not everyone was convinced that tomatoes were safe to eat. In 1820, Colonel Robert Johnson of Salem, New Jersey, set out to prove that they were.

At noon on September 26, Robert stood on the steps of the Salem courthouse. As a crowd of townspeople watched in silence, Robert bit into a ripe red tomato. A woman screamed and fainted, but nobody paid any attention to her. All eyes were on the colonel. He ate another tomato and raised his hands high, whereupon the crowd shouted, "He's alive! It's not poison!"

Today, tomatoes are not only safe to eat, but they are good for you, too! There are hundreds of different types, and they are one of the most popular homegrown vegetables *and* fruit. A tomato is a fruit because it develops from the ovary of the plant and contains seeds. A tomato is considered a vegetable because we don't usually eat it as dessert. (Try the Tomato Cake on page 103.)

- The first tomato sauce recipe appeared in Italy in 1692.

- Tomatoes can relieve insomnia, and tomato juice, blended with basil, can ease a headache.

- The different pronunciations of "tomato" were popularized by songwriters George and Ira Gershwin in their 1937 tune "Let's Call the Whole Thing Off": "You like to-may-to and I like to-mah-to."

- The first tomato ketchup recipe in the United States appeared in 1801 in the *Sugar House Book*.

- A tomato "tree" from China produces over 1,000 pounds of golf ball–size tomatoes every year at Disney World's Epcot theme park in Florida.

Start With Seedlings

1 When there is no danger of a frost, plant homegrown or store-bought seedlings in compost (rich soil) in a sunny garden or pot. (Use a pot that is at least 20 inches in diameter and holds at least 12 inches of soil for the roots.)

2 Lift the seedling carefully from the container and set it into a hole deep enough to have the top leaves and 1 inch of stem above the ground. (If you used peat pots, put the entire pot into the hole.)

3 Spread mulch around the plants and water them regularly.

SPREAD THE RED

Around the base of your tomatoes, spread red plastic. (Get it in garden stores, or cut up plastic tablecloths from dollar stores.) Red plastic reflects red light onto the underside of the leaves, which causes the plants to grow larger and bear more fruit.

What did Mama Tomato say to Baby Tomato when he lagged behind?

Ketchup!

The Secret, Symbolic Meanings of Flowers

The plant name is above the picture; its meaning is below.

DANDELION

Sympathy

WHITE CLOVER

Think of me

DAISY

Patience

LAVENDER

Devotion

IRIS

Wisdom

GLADIOLUS

Strength

LILAC

Pride

NASTURTIUM

Patriotism

RED POPPY

Consolation

PANSY

Thinking of you

GERANIUM

Friendship

YELLOW VIOLET

Happiness

ROSE

Love

SWEET PEA

Pleasure

SUNFLOWER

Adoration

PEAS, PLEASE

Peas are ANCIENT!

- Wild peas found in Asia date from around 9000 B.C.
- Greeks and Romans were cultivating peas as early as 500 B.C.
- Dried peas have been found in ancient Egyptian tombs.

TODAY, there are hundreds of pea varieties to plant, so pick your pleasure:

Sweet peas have tough pods. To shell the peas, break off the stem with your fingers and pull the "string" the length of the pod. Gently squeeze the pod and it will open. Remove the peas and toss the pod into the compost heap.

Sugar snap peas have tender pods that can be eaten raw or cooked, with the peas inside.

Snow peas have the thinnest and most tender pods and can be eaten raw or cooked, pod and all.

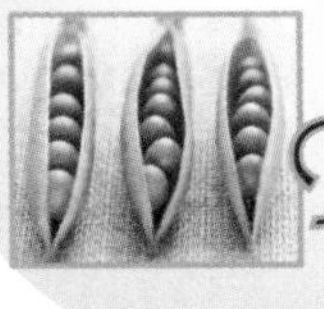

The smaller the peas, the more to the pot.

–proverb

CONTINUED

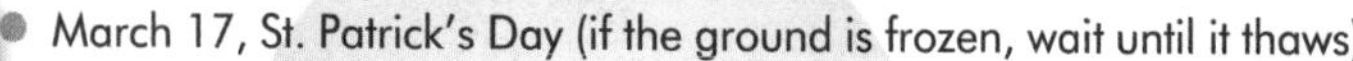

Peas like cool weather. Traditional times for planting peas are . . .

- March 17, St. Patrick's Day (if the ground is frozen, wait until it thaws)
- when lilacs show their first leaves
- when daffodils begin to bloom

Plant seeds 2 to 3 inches apart, about 1 inch deep, in rows about 1 foot apart, in loose soil that drains well. Give the tiny plants something to climb, such as thin sticks or tree branches stuck in the ground. Water regularly and remove any weeds. Pea roots are short, so be gentle when pulling weeds or cut weeds with scissors at ground level.

When the plants start to produce pods, pick them every 2 to 3 days. If you have waited too long and the pods have become tough, shell the peas and discard the pods. Cook the peas briefly in boiling water (ask an adult for help).

GREEN THUMB

The expression "green thumb" may have originated during the reign of King Edward I of England. He was fond of green peas and kept half a dozen serfs (servants) shelling them during the season. The serf who had the greenest thumb won a prize.

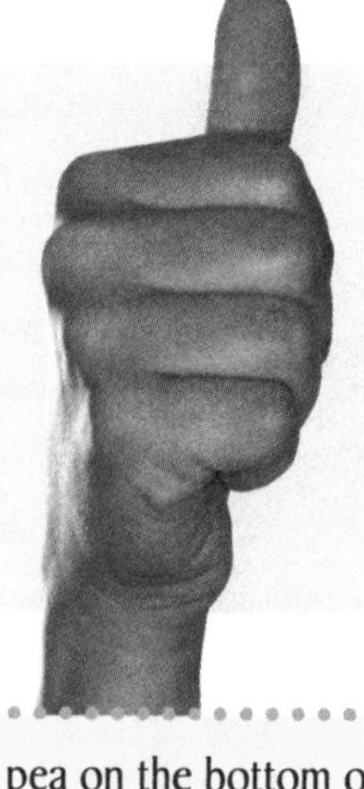

ROYAL PEA

A LONG TIME AGO, a prince was searching for a true princess to marry. One day, a girl claiming to be a princess came to the castle. The queen invited the girl to spend the night because she wanted to test her. The queen placed a pea on the bottom of the guest bed and then piled 20 mattresses and 20 feather beds on top.

The next morning, the queen asked the girl how she had slept. "I couldn't sleep at all," she said. "There was something hard in the bed, and this

Pea-lieve It OR NOT

- **Peas** were a bedtime snack for royalty in 17th-century France.
- Thomas Jefferson, third president of the United States, planted 30 varieties of **peas** in his garden at Monticello.
- In 2010, Ron Sveden of Brewster, Massachusetts, was found to have a **pea** growing in his lung. The pea sprout was ½-inch long.
- Janet Harris of Sussex, England, holds the world record for eating **peas.** In 1984, she ate 7,175 peas, one by one, in 60 minutes—using chopsticks!
- Peas return nitrogen to the soil, so farmers often grow their **peas** in a different place each year.

Lucky Peas

It's lucky to find only one pea in a pod.

If you find nine peas in a pod, throw one over your right shoulder and make a wish.

morning I'm covered with bruises."

This convinced the prince and his mother that the girl was honest, for only a real princess could be so sensitive.

–adapted from "The Princess and the Pea" by Hans Christian Andersen, Danish writer (1835–75)

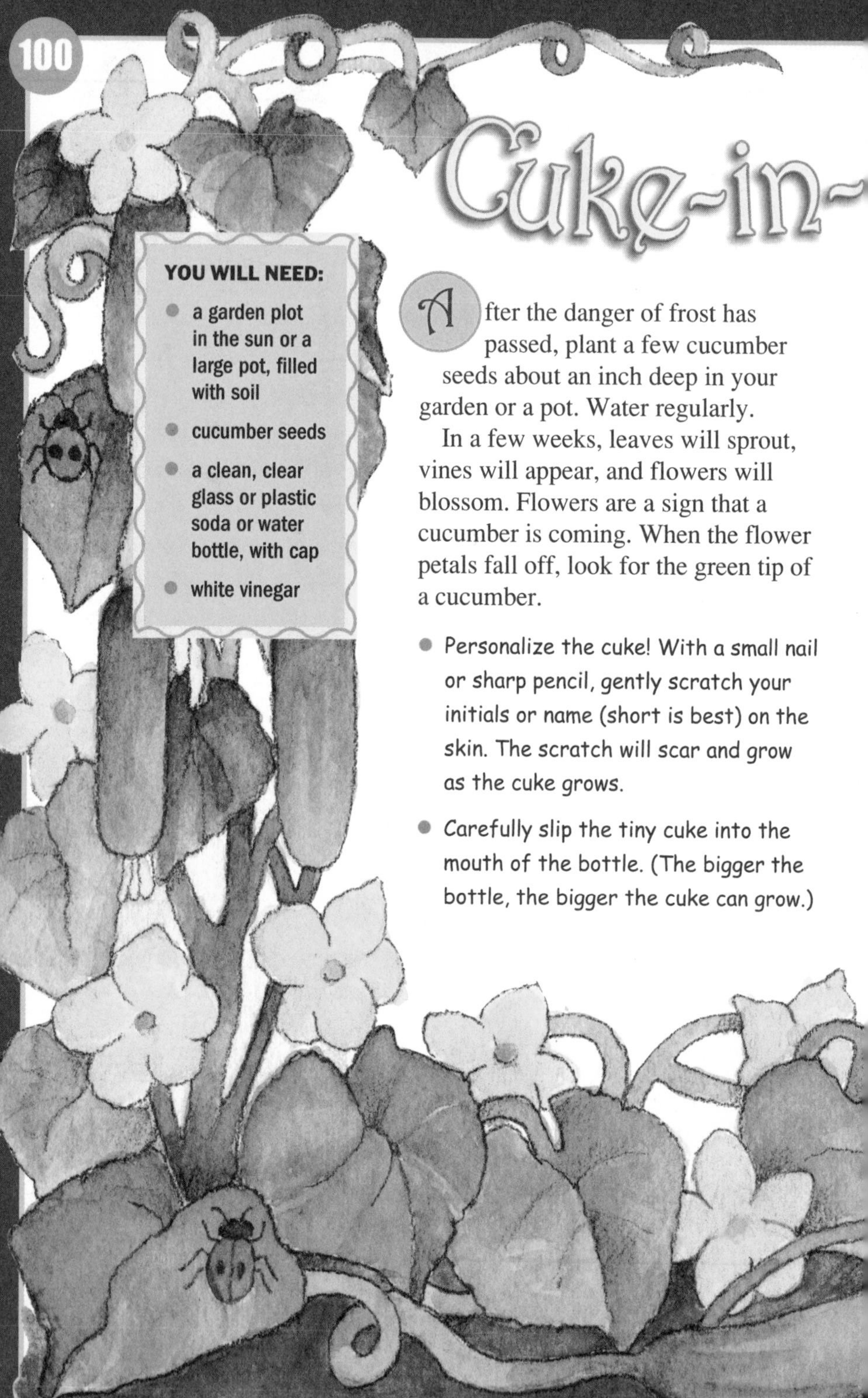

Cuke-in-

YOU WILL NEED:

- a garden plot in the sun or a large pot, filled with soil
- cucumber seeds
- a clean, clear glass or plastic soda or water bottle, with cap
- white vinegar

After the danger of frost has passed, plant a few cucumber seeds about an inch deep in your garden or a pot. Water regularly.

In a few weeks, leaves will sprout, vines will appear, and flowers will blossom. Flowers are a sign that a cucumber is coming. When the flower petals fall off, look for the green tip of a cucumber.

- Personalize the cuke! With a small nail or sharp pencil, gently scratch your initials or name (short is best) on the skin. The scratch will scar and grow as the cuke grows.
- Carefully slip the tiny cuke into the mouth of the bottle. (The bigger the bottle, the bigger the cuke can grow.)

a-Bottle

- Rest the bottle on the soil.
- Shade the bottle with an umbrella or newspaper so that the cuke doesn't cook in the midday sun.

Continue watering the plant regularly. The cucumber will grow inside the bottle. Any other cucumbers that grow will be yours to eat.

When the cucumber almost fills the bottle, cut it off the vine.

Fill the bottle with water, then drain it. This will rinse the cucumber and remove any dirt. Fill the bottle with white vinegar to preserve the cucumber, and then cap the bottle. Keep it in the refrigerator when you are not showing it off.

Two Bottle Trees

Some trees that belong to the cacao (or chocolate) tree family have trunks that grow in the shape of bottles. These "bottle trees" are native to Australia.

People in southern states sometimes make "bottle trees" by putting empty colored bottles on the ends of branches. According to folklore, the bottles trap any evil spirits that try to get into the owner's home.

Veggie SURPRISES

Each of these recipes contains a "hidden" vegetable. Ask an adult to help you make these. Then share with your friends and ask them to guess the vegetable.

TOMATO CAKE

- 1 cup dark-brown sugar
- ½ cup (1 stick) butter, softened
- 2 eggs
- 3 cups all-purpose flour
- 2 teaspoons baking powder
- 1 teaspoon baking soda
- 1 teaspoon nutmeg
- 1 teaspoon salt
- 2 cups fresh ripe tomatoes, peeled, seeded, and chopped or canned chopped tomatoes, drained
- ½ cup chopped walnuts
- ¾ cup chopped raisins

Preheat the oven to 350°F. Grease and flour a 13x9-inch baking pan. In a large bowl, mix the sugar and butter. Add the eggs and mix until well blended. Add the flour, baking powder, baking soda, nutmeg, and salt. Mix everything well. Stir in the tomatoes, nuts, and raisins. Pour the batter into the prepared pan. Bake the cake for 35 minutes, or until a toothpick inserted into the center comes out clean. Remove the pan from the oven and cool it on a rack. Remove the cake from the pan. Eat it plain or frost it with your favorite frosting.

MAKES 12 SERVINGS.

The heaviest tomato (so far!) was a 'Delicious' grown in Edmond, Oklahoma, in 1986. It weighed 7 pounds 12 ounces. Its vine was 53 feet 6 inches long.

continued

Palmer, Alaska, was home to one of the biggest beets ever grown. It weighed 42 pounds 12 ounces.

BEET SPICE CAKE

- 1¾ cups all-purpose flour
- ½ teaspoon baking powder
- ½ teaspoon baking soda
- 1 teaspoon salt
- 1 teaspoon ground allspice
- 1 cup sugar
- ½ cup vegetable oil
- 1 teaspoon vanilla extract
- 2 eggs
- 1 cup lightly packed shredded canned beets*
- ½ cup raisins
- ½ cup chopped walnuts

*This equals about half of a 16-ounce can of whole or medium beets.

Preheat the oven to 350°F. Grease an 8½x4½x2½-inch loaf pan. In a medium bowl, stir together the flour, baking powder, baking soda, salt, and allspice. In a large bowl, beat the sugar, oil, and vanilla until blended. Beat in the eggs, one at a time, until blended. Add the flour mixture one-third at a time, stirring after each until thoroughly combined. Add the beets, raisins, and walnuts and stir. Pour into the prepared loaf pan. Bake the cake for 1 hour, or until a toothpick inserted into the center comes out clean.

MAKES 8 TO 10 SERVINGS.

the not-so-neat BEET

- **To remove a beet stain from clothing,** soak a piece of white bread in cold water and put the bread on the stain. When the bread has absorbed the stain, wash the clothing as usual.
- **To remove beet stains from your fingers,** rub them briskly with salt and then wash them with soap and cool water. Repeat as needed.

ZUCCHINI BROWNIES

- 1 cup (2 sticks) butter
- ½ cup vegetable oil
- 1¾ cups sugar
- 2 eggs
- 1 teaspoon vanilla extract
- ½ cup milk, with 1 teaspoon lemon juice added to sour (let stand 5 minutes)
- 2½ cups all-purpose flour
- ¼ cup cocoa
- ½ teaspoon baking powder
- 1 teaspoon baking soda
- ½ teaspoon cinnamon
- ½ teaspoon ground cloves
- 2 cups shredded zucchini
- ⅔ cup chocolate chips

Preheat the oven to 325°F. Grease and flour a 13x9-inch baking pan. In a large bowl, cream together the butter, oil, and sugar. Add the eggs, vanilla, and sour milk, and beat until well blended.

In a separate bowl, mix the flour, cocoa, baking powder, baking soda, cinnamon, cloves, and zucchini. Add the dry ingredients to the egg mixture and stir until well-blended. Spread the batter in the prepared pan and sprinkle with chocolate chips. Bake for 40 minutes, or until a toothpick inserted into the center comes out clean. **MAKES 20 BROWNIES.**

One of the biggest zucchini ever grown weighed 64 pounds 8 ounces. It was cultivated in the United Kingdom.

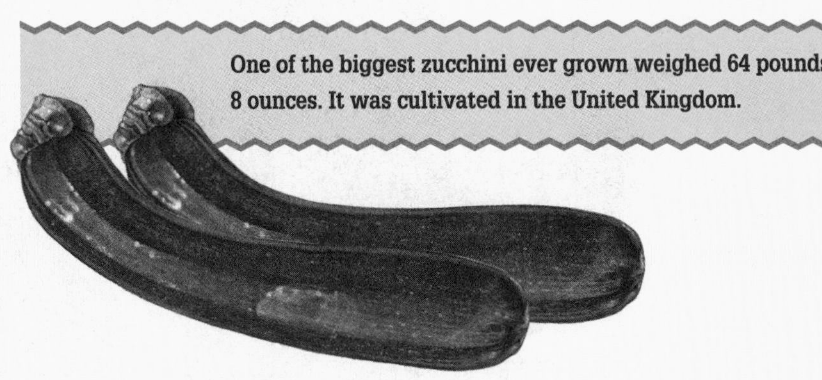

This ALLIGATOR Grows On a TREE

It's not an animal. It's not a vegetable. It's an AVOCADO!

Avocados are called **alligator pears** because they have rough, green skin like alligators and are shaped like pears. The fruit have such a smooth, creamy texture that they were once eaten only by royalty.

The avocado tree originated in south-central Mexico, sometime between 7000 and 5000 B.C. Archaeologists in Peru discovered avocado seeds buried with Incan mummies that date from 750 B.C. Today, people all over the world enjoy them in many different ways, such as in salads, sushi, soup, candy, guacamole—even in ice cream in Brazil!

DID YOU KNOW?

- The avocado is a berry.
- The tree is an evergreen. It can grow 30 to 80 feet tall.
- An avocado pit (its seed) makes up 10 to 25 percent of the fruit's weight.

Call Him MR. AVOCADO

About 80 percent of the avocados eaten today can be traced to a special "mother tree."

In the late 1920s, a postman named Rudolph Hass bought avocado seeds from A. R. Rideout of Whittier, California. Rudy planted the seeds and tried to graft some other varieties onto a tree that grew from one of them. When the grafts didn't work, Rudy planned to cut the tree down. A friend persuaded him to keep the tree because it appeared to be strong and healthy.

That tree produced a lot of avocados, and in 1935, Rudy took out a patent, giving the variety his last name: Hass avocados. He also made a deal with a fruit farmer to grow and promote his avocados.

Rudy's plan was a great success. People liked the rich, nutty taste of Hass avocados, and grocers realized that these avocados didn't spoil as quickly as other varieties.

Rudy Hass died in 1952, but that first Hass tree survived until 2002, when root fungus killed it. Today, its descendants are all over the world.

One avocado tree can produce as many as 500 avocados (or 200 pounds of fruit) per year. An average harvest from one tree is about 150 avocados (60 pounds).

The oldest known living avocado tree is on the campus of the University of California, Berkeley. It was planted in 1879.

Avocado oil is used in sunscreens, skin moisturizers, hair conditioners, and makeup.

CONTINUED

Grow Your Own AVOCADO TREE

- Ask an adult to help you remove the pit from an avocado. Eat the flesh. Wash the pit and allow it to dry for 2 to 3 days.

- Stick three toothpicks into the pit's equator (or middle), equidistant apart and about ½-inch deep. Place the pit, with its fat base down, on the rim of a water glass, using the toothpicks to suspend it so that it doesn't fall into the glass. Add enough water to the glass to cover about an inch of the pit.

- Put the glass in a warm place out of direct sunlight. Add more water as needed. Roots and a stem should sprout in 2 to 6 weeks.

- When the stem is 6 to 7 inches long, cut it back to about 3 inches.

- When the roots are thick and the stem has grown out again, plant it in potting soil in an 8- to 10-inch-diameter pot, leaving the pit half exposed.

- Set the pot in a sunny spot. Water the tree often, lightly, keeping the soil moist but not soaking wet. (Yellow leaves are a sign of too much water.) When the tree is about a foot high, cut it back to 6 inches so that new shoots will sprout.

- Your tree can live outside in the summer. Bring it indoors if winter temperatures go below 45°F. Be patient! It may take 10 to 15 years for your tree to begin producing fruit.

Breakfast, Lunch, or Dinner

Avocado tastes great by itself, in salads, or spread on bread anytime. On special occasions or if you grow your own, try these treats.

Avocado Shake

This is a popular summer drink in Brazil.

½ avocado, peeled and pitted
1½ cups milk
½ cup ice
3 tablespoons sugar

Put the ingredients into a blender. Process the mixture on high for about 1 minute. Pour it into a glass and enjoy! **Makes 1 serving.**

Guacamole

Serve this popular Mexican dip with tortilla chips.

2 avocados, peeled and pitted
1 tablespoon lime juice
½ tomato, chopped, or desired amount of salsa
¼ teaspoon salt

Put the avocado flesh into a bowl and mash it. Add the remaining ingredients and stir to combine. **Makes 4 to 6 servings.**

Avocado Mousse

This is almost good enough for breakfast—but better for dessert.

3 avocados, peeled and pitted
juice of 2 limes, freshly squeezed
½ cup sweetened whipped cream

Put the avocado flesh and lime juice into a blender and process on high until smooth. Put the mixture into a large bowl, add the whipped cream, and gently stir until most of the cream is light green. **Makes 2 to 4 servings.**

WELCOME A RABBLE* OF BUTTERFLIES

Every year, more than 700 species look for a home. How about yours?

***the term for a group or swarm of butterflies**

Get a Garden Going

Butterflies look for plants that provide food and offer a place to lay eggs. Their favorite food is nectar, a sweet secretion produced by certain flowering plants. Butterflies also prefer plants with . . .

- daisylike petals on which to perch
- blooms large enough for the butterfly to insert its proboscis (strawlike feeding tube) to draw out the nectar
- blooms in clusters, providing a nectar buffet

1

Butterflies love the following plants, which flower at different times and grow to differing heights. Use a variety of them in a sunny spot.

1 daisy
2 aster
3 garden or meadow phlox
4 sunflower
5 pink, purple, or Tennessee coneflower
6 verbena

2

4

5

3

6

Many butterflies lay their eggs on the underside of a leaf or on a stem, choosing host plants that will provide food for the caterpillars that will emerge from the eggs. There are almost as many hosts as there are butterfly species.

HERE ARE A FEW PAIRINGS

Butterfly	Host Plants
checkered skipper	hollyhock, mallow
common buckeye	snapdragon, plantain
northern blue	lupine, pea
painted lady	sunflower, hollyhock
question mark	nettle, hackberry

CONTINUED

Serve Stinky Snacks

Many butterflies love to sip juice from rotten fruit—almost any fruit will do:

apples	nectarines
bananas	pawpaws
berries	pears
cantaloupes	persimmons
figs	tomatoes
grapes	watermelons

To serve butterfly snacks, screw or nail a plastic dinner plate to a flat-top post in a shady spot. Place some rotten fruit on the plate and watch for butterflies. (Other insects and critters might nibble on it, too.)

When the butterflies are finished, toss the remains into a compost heap and wash the plate with a garden hose.

MILKWEED, a Butterfly Magnet

Monarch butterflies suck up the flower nectar of MILKWEED, and the caterpillars eat the plant's milky sap, or latex. The sap eaten by the caterpillars is passed along during metamorphosis. It protects monarch butterflies by being poisonous to their insect and bird enemies. A bird that eats a monarch butterfly will vomit immediately because of the sap!

LOOK, DON'T TOUCH: Milkweed sap can cause skin irritation, and eating it can make you violently ill.

Make a Splash

- Butterflies are attracted to pools of water that are up to a foot deep—a butterfly's foot, that is! On a hot day, place a few smooth stones and some gravel in a saucer. Add enough water to wet but not cover the stones. Butterflies will perch on the stones and sip the water.

Bring a Butterfly to LIFE

YOU WILL NEED:

- **a washed glass or plastic jar**
- **clear plastic kitchen wrap and a rubber band, for a lid**
- **a stick that fits inside the jar**
- **a caterpillar**
- **fresh leaves from the caterpillar's favorite food plant**

Capture a feeding caterpillar **(1)** and put it into the jar with a few leaves from the plant you found it on. Set the stick in the jar for the caterpillar to use as it turns into a pupa, or chrysalis **(2)**. Cover the jar with the plastic wrap, secured by the rubber band, and poke some air holes in it. Add fresh leaves daily.

When the chrysalis is completely formed **(3)**, remove the leaves. Check the chrysalis daily, watching for it to change color.

As the butterfly emerges from the chrysalis **(4)**, do not touch its wings.

Carefully carry the container outside and remove the lid. Let the butterfly crawl up the stick to dry and harden its wings—and then fly free!

Read about and see photos of one editor's experience with raising a caterpillar and share yours at **Almanac4kids.com.**

This is Really CORNY

A CORNUCOPIA OF FACTS ABOUT

The Vegetable That Grows on an Ear

Keep the Kernels Straight

DENT CORN, named for the little dent that appears on each side of a kernel when it dries, is grown to feed cows and chickens. Nearly 60 percent of all of the corn grown in the United States is dent corn.

SWEET CORN is the type that people eat.

FLOUR CORN is used to make flour for baking.

FLINT CORN kernels have a hard exterior. They are often ground up to be used as feed for livestock. The white, yellow, red, and dark blue kernels (sometimes all on one ear!) are also used for decorations.

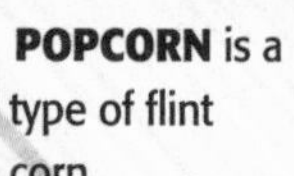

POPCORN is a type of flint corn.

GET GROWING

With an adult, choose a sunny area of the garden with well-drained soil. After all danger of frost has passed, mark off an area about 6x6 feet. Make four rows running from east (where the Sun rises) to west (where the Sun sets). In each row, make holes 6 to 7 inches apart and about 2 inches deep. Put a corn seed (kernel) into each hole.

FIELDWORK

Corn is grown in blocks because wind carries the pollen from the tassels of one stalk to the silk of another plant nearby. Sometimes farmers walk through the rows early in the morning and gently shake the stalks to set free the pollen.

CONTINUED

Water and weed the corn regularly. To know when to water, dig down about 2 inches. If the soil is dry, water.

Corn grows slowly until it reaches about 24 inches. Then it takes off, growing 3 to 4 inches per day during hot weather. Plus, the roots of the plant grow as much as the leaves.

When it's time to harvest . . .

Sweet Corn

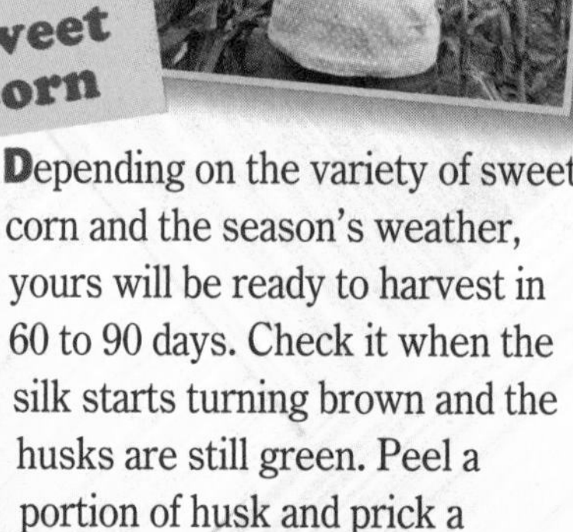

Depending on the variety of sweet corn and the season's weather, yours will be ready to harvest in 60 to 90 days. Check it when the silk starts turning brown and the husks are still green. Peel a portion of husk and prick a kernel. If milky liquid comes out, the corn is ready to be picked. If the liquid is clear, the corn is immature. If there is no liquid, the kernels are dry and it's too late.

Popcorn

Leave the ears on the stalks until the husks are dry and the corn kernels are hard. Then, harvest the ears, pull off the husks, put the cobs into mesh bags, and hang the bags to dry in a warm, ventilated place. Pick off a few kernels once or twice a week and try popping them. If they pop well and taste good, the corn is ready. If the popcorn is chewy, dry the cobs longer.

To remove dried popcorn kernels from the cob, rub two ears of corn together. The kernels will fall off. Or, hold an ear of corn with both hands and twist it. (Do this over a bucket or pot.) Leave the small kernels at the tip of the ear; they won't make good popcorn.

Store dried kernels in clean, airtight containers.

Tops in Pops

Choose a variety of popcorn that is suitable to your climate. 'Japanese Hull-less' will grow almost anywhere; it matures in about 85 days and pops very well. Or, try growing 'Ruby Red' or 'Miniature Blue', with their colorful kernels.

FIELDWORK

Popcorn and sweet corn must be grown in separate gardens far away from each other. If they are close, they can cross-pollinate and produce sweet corn kernels with a hard exterior and bland taste.

A "POP" QUIZ: Why Does Corn Pop?

Folklore

Some Native American tribes believed that each kernel was a home for a spirit. When the kernel was heated, the spirits would get angry and begin to shake. When they couldn't stand it any longer, they popped out of their kernel and drifted away as a puff of steam.

Fact

Corn pops when water in the kernel is heated. As heat increases pressure in the kernel, it turns inside out, or pops.

CONTINUED

POPCORN BALLS

YOU WILL NEED:

- 16 cups popped popcorn
- ½ cup sugar
- ½ cup dark corn syrup
- butter, for greasing your hands

Put the popcorn in a very large bowl. Put the sugar and corn syrup in a saucepan. Cook on medium heat and stir until the sugar is just dissolved. (Ask an adult for help.) Remove the pan from the heat and pour the mixture over the popcorn. Stir the popcorn gently until it is evenly coated. Rub butter on your hands. Gently form the popcorn mixture into balls by hand. Wrap each in cellophane wrap or waxed paper.

MAKES ABOUT 1 DOZEN BALLS.

DID YOU KNOW?

An **EAR OF CORN** has, on average, 800 kernels, 16 rows, and 50 kernels in each row. There is one strand of corn silk for each kernel.

Corn, or corn products, such as **CORNSTARCH, CORN SYRUP,** or **CORN FLOUR,** are used in many foods, including cookies, cakes, soda, candy bars, and yogurt.

Most of the corn in the United States is grown in a 13-state area called the **CORN BELT.** Four of these states—Illinois, Iowa, Minnesota, and Nebraska—produce 50 percent of the corn.

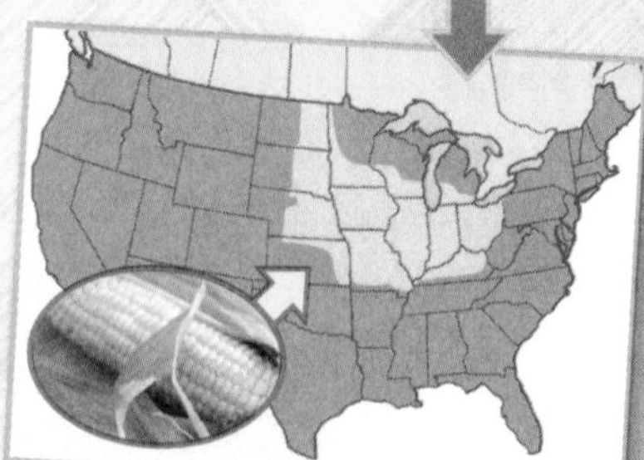

In the 1970s, Professor Walton Galinat bred the first corn for the Jet Age. Each flat ear had two rows of kernels. It was jokingly called **"AIRPLANE CORN"** because it would not roll off a food tray on a plane, no matter how much turbulence the plane encountered.

Mitchell, South Dakota, is home to the world's only **CORN PALACE.** Its exterior is decorated with corn, grains, and grasses. Each year, new decorations are made for the Corn Palace Festival.

Nuggets

Some people don't think these tales are true! (Do you?)

A Headless Chicken

Mike the chicken lost his head on September 10, 1945, when his owner, farmer Lloyd Olsen, chopped it off, intending for Mike to become Sunday dinner. Mike began running around. (Beheaded chickens sometimes do that.) So Lloyd left Mike for a while.

An hour later, Lloyd noticed that Mike was strutting around normally with all of the other chickens, preening his feathers and even attempting to peck for food—unsuccessfully, of course.

The next morning, Lloyd found Mike still alive, sleeping with what was left of his neck tucked under his wing. Lloyd decided that Mike was special and tried feeding him grain and water with an eyedropper inserted down his esophagus. It worked fine.

A week later, Lloyd took Mike to the University of Utah in Salt Lake City, where scientists drew three conclusions:

- Lloyd's ax blade had partially missed Mike's jugular vein.
- The remainder of that vein had clotted.
- Part of Mike's brain stem and one ear remained on his body. Apparently that was enough, the doctors declared, to sustain Mike's life. (Most of Mike's head was in a glass jar back at the Olsen farm.)

continued

Over the next 18 months, the Olsens took Mike on a national tour. People everywhere lined up to pay 25 cents to see him. He seemed healthy (gaining 8 pounds) and happy.

Then, one night in a motel in Arizona, Mike began choking. When the Olsens couldn't find the eyedropper to clear Mike's throat, he finally died. Too bad, because some people felt that with proper care (even without a head), he might have lived practically forever.

In Mike's Memory

Every May, the town of Fruita, Colorado, holds a "do" on the third weekend in May to celebrate the life of Mike, the chicken who not only lived, but thrived, without his head.

The Head Chicken

In the 1950s, a major airline hired a veterinary surgeon to study animal behavior in flight. The doctor learned that elephants that travel in pairs keep their own company and that a white chicken is a good companion for an elephant traveling by itself. (Elephants have poor eyesight, but a white chicken is easy for an elephant to see.)

Thereafter, in the days before a flight, the poultry and pachyderm (another word for "elephant") would be "introduced" and become acquainted. On board, the chicken rode on the elephant's head. If the elephant became agitated while in the air and stomped around, an attendant would tie the chicken on a leash to one of the elephant's legs. Fearful of stepping on his little buddy, the elephant would once again stand steady and enjoy the ride.

Why does a chicken coop have two doors?

Because if it had four doors, it would be a chicken sedan.

A Boy, a Bracelet, and a Broiler

When Aaron Giles was a child, he played with his brothers and sisters on his grandfather's farm in Fairmont, Minnesota. Aaron wore a small metal identification bracelet on which was engraved his name, address, and phone number. One day, while playing, he lost the bracelet.

More than 25 years later, in 2007, while preparing chickens for market, a meat cutter found a bracelet in a chicken's gizzard (part of its digestive system). All of the engravings on the bracelet were legible—it was Aaron's!

The meat cutter found Aaron's father and returned the bracelet to his son. No one knows exactly where or when the chicken swallowed the bracelet.

FOWL FACTS

- **Alektorophobia is extreme fear of live chickens.**
- Ameraucana and Araucana chickens lay blue or green eggs.
- **China has more than 3 billion chickens. The United States has about 450 million.**
- The disease "chicken pox" has nothing to do with poultry. The name comes from the Old English term "gican pox," which means itchy pox.
- **Chickens can fly up to 9 miles per hour.**
- **If burned, the poop that a chicken makes in its lifetime could supply enough electricity to run a 100-watt light bulb for 5 hours.**
- The largest recorded chicken egg weighed almost 12 ounces and measured 12¼ inches around.

Q: What day of the week do chickens hate most?

A: Fry day.

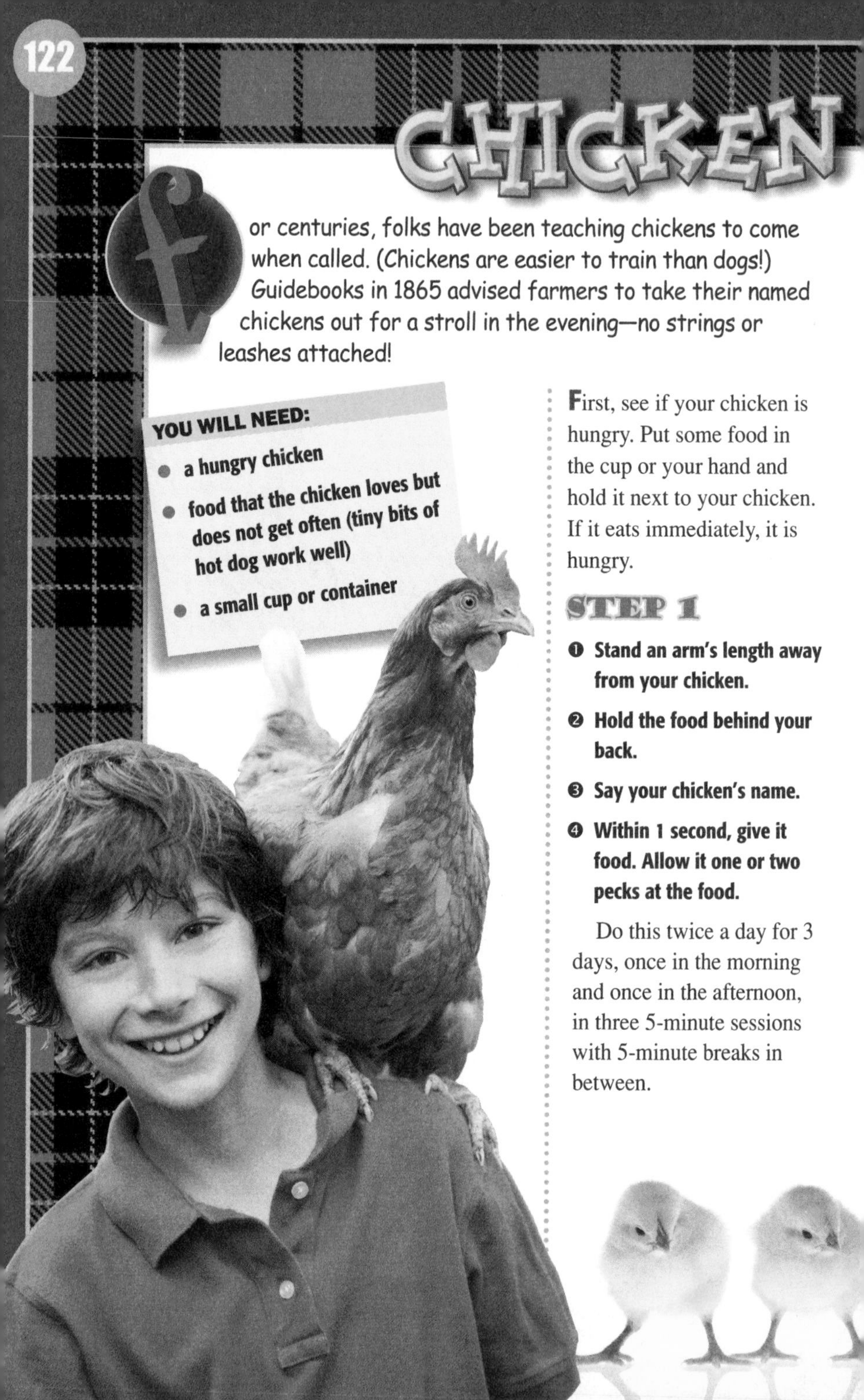

CHICKEN

For centuries, folks have been teaching chickens to come when called. (Chickens are easier to train than dogs!) Guidebooks in 1865 advised farmers to take their named chickens out for a stroll in the evening—no strings or leashes attached!

YOU WILL NEED:

- **a hungry chicken**
- **food that the chicken loves but does not get often (tiny bits of hot dog work well)**
- **a small cup or container**

First, see if your chicken is hungry. Put some food in the cup or your hand and hold it next to your chicken. If it eats immediately, it is hungry.

STEP 1

1. **Stand an arm's length away from your chicken.**
2. **Hold the food behind your back.**
3. **Say your chicken's name.**
4. **Within 1 second, give it food. Allow it one or two pecks at the food.**

Do this twice a day for 3 days, once in the morning and once in the afternoon, in three 5-minute sessions with 5-minute breaks in between.

TRAINING 101

STEP 2

1. **Stand about an arm's length away from your chicken.**
2. **Hold the food behind your back. When your chicken is looking away from you, say its name.**
3. **Give it food immediately.**

It will start to associate its name with food and look toward you and the food whenever you say its name.

STEP 3

1. **Stand several feet away from your chicken.**
2. **Call your chicken's name and offer it the food at the same time.**

It should run right over.

WING IT

Once your chicken masters Steps 1, 2, and 3, add distractions to test it. Practice in a new location or scatter its regular food on the ground when it knows that you have treats.

If you call it and it ignores you, it's not hungry or is confused by the distraction. Do not keep calling it, or it will learn to ignore you. Instead, decrease the distraction and try again when it is hungry.

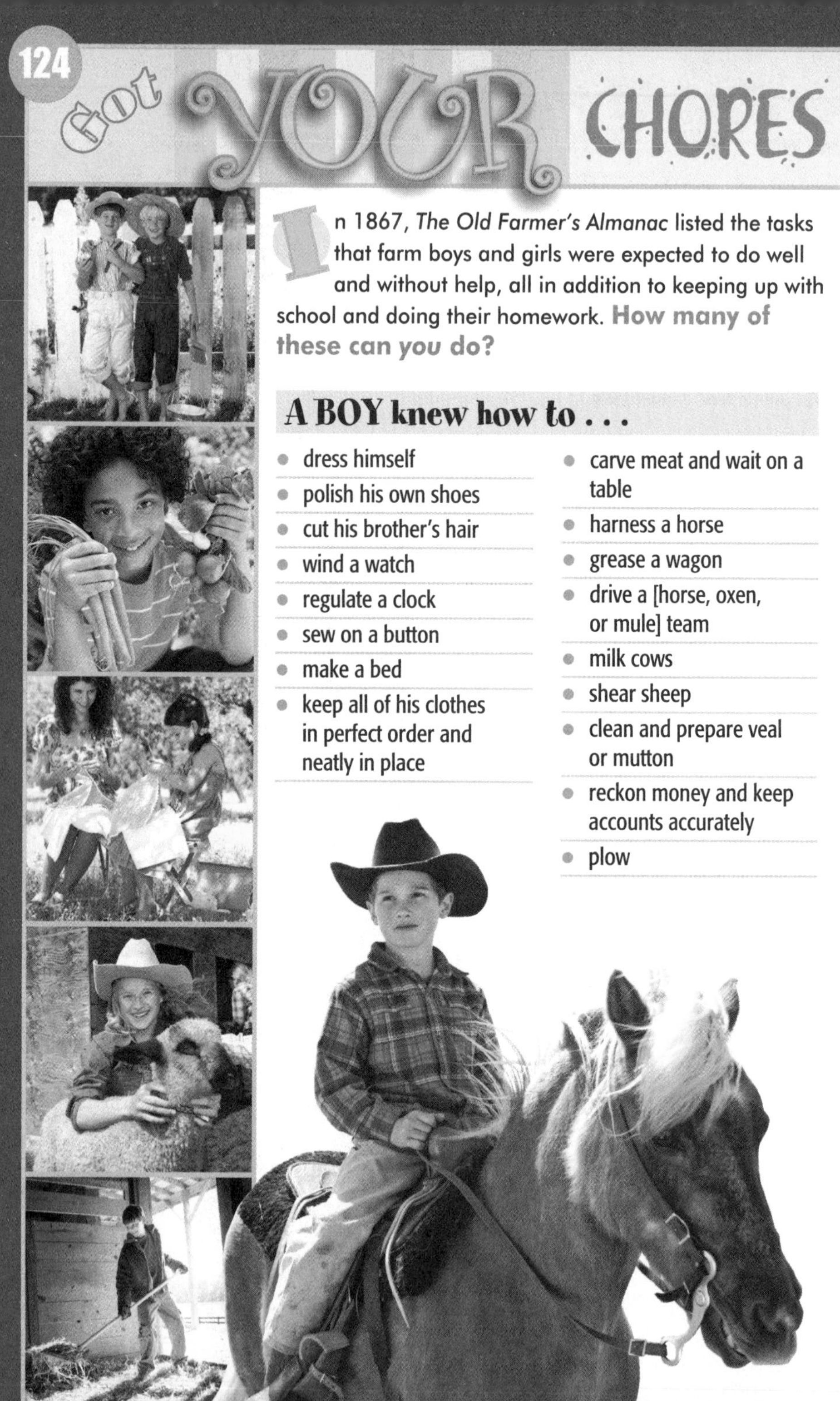

Got YOUR CHORES

In 1867, *The Old Farmer's Almanac* listed the tasks that farm boys and girls were expected to do well and without help, all in addition to keeping up with school and doing their homework. **How many of these can *you* do?**

A BOY knew how to . . .

- dress himself
- polish his own shoes
- cut his brother's hair
- wind a watch
- regulate a clock
- sew on a button
- make a bed
- keep all of his clothes in perfect order and neatly in place
- carve meat and wait on a table
- harness a horse
- grease a wagon
- drive a [horse, oxen, or mule] team
- milk cows
- shear sheep
- clean and prepare veal or mutton
- reckon money and keep accounts accurately
- plow

DONE?

- write a letter neatly and fold and address it properly
- write contracts
- pack and send a package
- sow grain and grass seed
- drive a mowing machine
- swing a scythe
- build a neat haystack
- pitch hay
- build a fire
- whitewash a wall
- mend broken tools

A GIRL knew how to . . .

- sew and knit
- work a sewing machine
- make dresses and children's clothes
- mend clothes neatly
- make a bed
- keep her room, closets, and drawers neatly in order
- dress her own hair
- wash dishes and sweep carpets
- trim and light lamp wicks
- bake good bread
- perform all basic cooking
- make good butter and cheese
- keep accounts and calculate interest
- write, fold, and address letters properly
- nurse the sick efficiently and not faint at the sight of a drop of blood
- aid and comfort those in trouble
- receive and entertain visitors when her mother was sick or absent

Advice for Any Time

The ability to take care of oneself is worth more than $100,000. In any trouble or difficulty, a boy or girl who can take care of him- or herself will have two excellent servants ready—their two hands. Learn to do as many different useful things as possible.

–*The Old Farmer's Almanac,* 1867

What skills—old or new—should kids have today? Share your ideas with other kids at **Almanac4kids.com/TellUs.**

- **A male burro is a JACK.**
- **A female burro is a JENNY.**

HEEE-HAWW . . .

That's the bray of a burro, or wild donkey. At 5 o'clock each morning at a farm in Connecticut, two burros sound off. Their raucous blasts mean, "We're hungry, feed us!" Owner Aldo Biagiotti does exactly that.

Aldo's two adopted burros arrived in a horse

A Tale of TWO

Dudley (left) and Reginold found a happy new home in Connecticut.

trailer. Scrawny and scared, they were at the end of a long journey from Death Valley, California. When Aldo lowered the trailer's tailgate, the burros balked at descending. With a little urging, they stepped slowly down the ramp. Then, tails switching and long ears twitching, the burros moved cautiously into their new surroundings. Soon they drifted about leisurely and nibbled idly on the grass.

Aldo named the donkeys **Reginold** and **Dudley.** Reginold is the aggressive, trusting, dominant burro. Dudley is gentle, quiet, and shy. Each one stands about 48 inches (12 hands) tall and weighs 400 pounds.

BURROS

How Burros Went Wild—and Then Into Homes

During the California gold rush, many prospectors transported their gear and grub to the goldfields on the backs of domestic donkeys. When the gold rush ended around 1855 and the prospectors had no need for their donkeys, they released them. During the same period, many donkeys belonging to the U.S. Cavalry, ranchers, explorers, and Native Americans escaped or were set free. All of these animals headed for the deserts, hills, and mountains and eventually became wild.

The wild donkeys multiplied and became too numerous for the government and private landowners to tend. Many ended up being slaughtered, which made a lot of people angry.

In 1973, the U.S. government started the Adopt-a-Burro program. Wild burros are rounded up and examined and treated by veterinarians. Healthy burros are placed with responsible citizens. Since the program began, more than 35,000 burros have been placed throughout the United States.

CONTINUED

Once you earn their trust, burros like to be

Reginold and Dudley arrive at Casa di Campagna farm.

As Aldo and the burros became acquainted, he learned how to behave around them. For example, on the second day, he opened the metal gate to the corral and let the donkeys out. Then, with an empty plastic bucket in hand, he walked behind them down to the pond. Suddenly, on hearing a noise, Reginold kicked his hind hooves backward and sent the bucket flying. Now, Aldo never walks close behind the burros.

Once you earn their trust, burros like to be hugged, petted, and talked to. Aldo sometimes wraps one arm around a donkey's neck and, with his free hand, scratches between its long ears. The burro nuzzles him like a small child would. However, when a strong wind blows, the burros become jittery, defensive, and unpredictable, and he is careful around them.

Aldo gives Dudley a hug.

Aldo speaks Italian to the burros. Now they understand that language as well as English. "*Buon giorno* [Good day], Reginold; *buon giorno*, Dudley," he says in the morning. On hearing him, the donkeys step out of the wooden shed. "*Andiamo* [Let's go]," he says, while opening the metal gate. Slowly, the burros come out and wander down to the pond, where they graze, drink, and rest.

Time for a stroll around the pond . . .

Later, he claps his hands and calls out, "Reginold! Dudley!" They approach the split-rail fence with

hugged, petted, and talked to.

Hands Up!

- A burro's height is measured in "hands." One hand equals 4 inches. The measurement is taken at the withers, the highest point of a burro's shoulder. Wild burros are 11 hands tall, on average.

hopes for a snack—and he has one: a sugar lump in the flat of his hand. (If he doesn't hold his hand flat, they nip his fingertips. Ouch!) One bite, and the sugar's gone.

When the burros are tired, they lie down in the dirt at the edge of the pond. Sometimes they roll back and forth, getting dusty and crushing bothersome flies and insects. The dust in the burros' fur discourages other flies and insects and insulates them from summer heat and winter cold.

In one day, Reginold and Dudley together eat a 40-pound bale of hay that contains alfalfa, timothy grass, and clover. Between them, they drink from 10 to 15 gallons of water. Twice a day, Aldo measures a coffee can full of a molasses and corn mixture for each burro. Occasionally, he tosses in cornstalks, which they love, and treats them to saltine crackers and carrots.

Burros enjoy being useful. Reginold and Dudley pull small wagons and carriages. In summer, they "cut" the lawn better than a lawn mower by eating the fresh grass.

. . . and time to play for a while.

As the Sun sets, Aldo opens the metal gate to the corral and the burros come up from the paddock for the night. Soon, they disappear into the shed. "*Buona notte* [Good night]," he says to each one. Walking back to the farmhouse, he thinks of how lucky he is.

SAINT BERNARDS: The Lovable Life

This giant breed has SUPER POWER:

- Its broad chest measures 26 to 30 inches at the shoulder.
- It weighs between 120 to 200 pounds at maturity.
- It has one and a half times the strength of the average dog.

The Saint Bernard dog is believed to be a descendant of mastiff-type dogs brought to Switzerland by the Romans between 1200 and 800 B.C. Swiss farmers called them *talhunde* ("valley dogs") or *bauernhunde* ("farm dogs"). With its natural ability for scent work, drafting, and pulling, the breed eventually became a loyal helper guarding property, herding sheep and cattle, and pulling wagons.

Around 1050, Archdeacon Bernard de Menthon built a hospice (rest stop) in the Alps for travelers who were navigating the treacherous mountain passes between Switzerland and Italy. Religious

savers TO THE RESCUE!

men called monks lived there and cared for ill or injured travelers.

Some monks who had grown up on farms thought that in winter a *talhund* (or two or three) would be a good companion that could help with chores. Soon, several dogs from nearby valleys were brought to the hospice. The breed eventually took on the name of the hospice's founder, who had become canonized as Saint Bernard.

Initially, the dogs did farmwork, but before long, their other natural abilities were discovered. Their chest and shoulder muscles enabled them to plow through deep snowdrifts. Their arched toes allowed them to tread easily on ice. Their broad tail balanced them when climbing.

The Saint Bernard is a NATURAL RESCUER.

- **It can make its way through snow as deep as 15 feet.**
- **Its nose contains 220 million smell receptors. (A human nose has 5 million.)**
- **It can hear high-pitched noises up to 47,000 hertz (cycles per second). (The human ear is most sensitive to frequencies around 1,000 hertz.)**
- **It can dig out a person buried as much as 7 feet lower than itself.**

- **It will often lie down beside a rescued victim to share its body heat. If the victim is unconscious, the dog will attempt revival by licking the person's face.**

CONTINUED

The monks began using the Saint Bernards to search for people who were lost or hurt in the Alps, especially in rough weather. The dogs performed so well that the monks trained them as pack animals and rescuers. The dogs wore a leather saddle that held blankets and medicine.

By 1750, the hospice had become home for 10 to 20 Saint Bernards that accompanied the monks on rescue and guide trips. As news of the dogs' work spread, travelers crossing the Great Saint Bernard Pass dropped by the hospice just to meet them.

DOGGED PURSUITS

Records at the Bernard de Menthon hospice indicate that the Saint Bernards made over 2,000 rescues (many more went unrecorded). Worldwide, they have saved and guided thousands . . .

1800 to 1814: "Barry" saved at least 40 lives, including that of a young boy stranded on an icy ledge that no man could climb. The boy awoke to the dog's warm licks, and Barry pulled him to safety.

In 1962, "Beggar" was named Dog Hero of the Year after he saved the life of a 3-year-old by pulling him out of a flooded river.

The HOSPICE and Its HEROES

Today, the dogs reside in a kennel in the valley, except between June 1 and October 15, when they are at the hospice. The rest stop remains active, and although the dogs no longer do much rescue work, the monks enjoy telling stories of past heroics to visitors year-round. Since its founding, the hospice doors have never been locked.

LEADERS OF THE PACKS

Other dogs commonly used for RESCUE MISSIONS include . . .

UNSUNG Animal Heroes

★★★★★

A Tail in Time

Henry G., traveling on horseback, stopped at a fork in a road near Plattsmouth, Nebraska. He dismounted in order to walk and turned his horse loose to follow him. The horse stopped to graze. After walking some distance, Henry sat down to wait for his mount to catch up.

Henry did not know that the road contained a patch of quicksand. The sign indicating the dangerous sinkhole was missing.

Time passed and the horse did not appear. Henry stirred and only then noticed that the sand firmly held his legs. He was slowly being drawn into the earth!

Henry shouted for help, but no one heard. He wondered what had happened to his horse. He called its name again and again, but it was too far away to hear him.

Henry sank deeper every minute. He heard a group of people singing "Home, Sweet Home" as they floated past in the nearby river and thought that he would never see his sweet home again.

The sand was up to his shoulders. He spread his arms to slow his sinking body.

Henry called to his horse repeatedly and whistled, too, hoping to get the animal's attention.

At last, the horse came running. By then, however, it was dark. The horse could not see Henry in the pit.

Desperate, Henry talked to his horse, giving it instructions.

Finally, the horse came and stood at the edge of the sand. Henry reached for the bridle, then the saddle, then the stirrup—but he was too low.

At that moment, the horse turned and Henry stretched and grabbed its tail. Struggling to hold on, he told the horse to go forward. The sand gripped him, yet after several minutes and an awful pull, Henry was dragged far enough away from the sand to rest and recover.

★★★★★

The Baby Saved by a Bird

Around 1890, a baby boy suddenly developed a swollen throat and fever. Upon discovering this, his mother became alarmed. Her husband, a member of the Pacific Coast Pigeon Society, was at his shop 5 miles away. What to do?

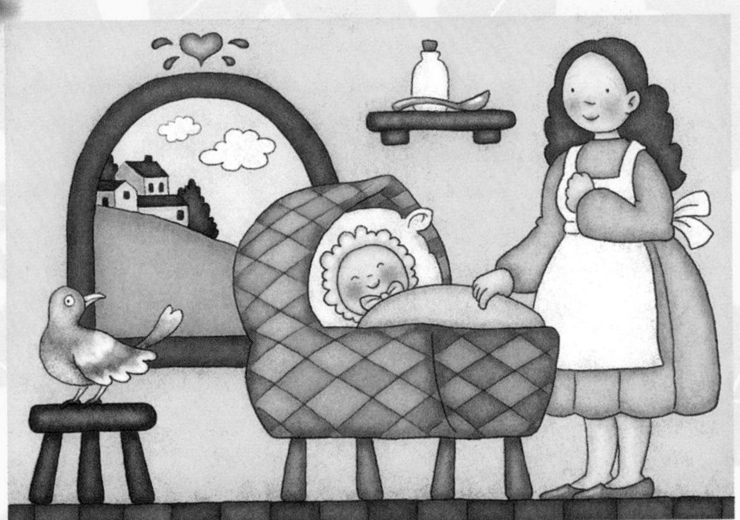

continued • • •

The distraught mother wrote a message describing their child's symptoms and pleading for medicine to save its life. She then tied the note onto the leg of one of her husband's carrier pigeons and dispatched it. (This is before telephones were in wide use.)

The bird flew swiftly and directly to the shop. The husband read the message, contacted a doctor, and explained the circumstances. The doctor prescribed the proper medicine. The husband acquired the medication, secured the vial to the pigeon, and sent the bird aloft. The pigeon sped for home, arriving in 10 minutes—more than four times faster than the the doctor would have been.

Thankfully, the medicine worked and the baby got well.

Paws for a Near Cat-astrophe

One evening, a train conductor found a yellow kitten sleeping on a seat. He carried the kitten to the engineer, who fed it, named it Dick, and put it in the baggage car for the night.

When the train went out the next day, Dick went with it. Dick was quite frightened at first but soon calmed down. After a few weeks, Dick began riding in the engine.

The engineer noticed that Dick was afraid of the sound of another train coming. He would crouch on the floor at the engineer's feet and remain there until the other train passed. For nearly a year, the engineer had tried in vain to break him of this.

On one trip, the train crew reached a station at 4:30 P.M. At about the same time, a freight train was due there from the opposite direction. Dick's crew waited 15 minutes for the freight. When it failed to appear, the conductor decided to go on to the next station 10 miles away. He telegraphed the agent at that station to tell him to hold the freight until he arrived. Receiving no message back, the conductor thought that it was safe to proceed and started Dick's train on its way.

It had gone about 5 miles when Dick suddenly raised his head, jumped to the floor, and crouched at his master's feet. The engineer thought that perhaps Dick heard the freight. He put his head out of the window and listened, but he could hear only the wind.

The engineer described Dick's behavior to the conductor, who ordered the train to stop and return to the last station. The engineer backed up at full speed.

Sure enough, 5 minutes after Dick's train arrived back in the station the late freight roared down the track. Both trains had narrowly escaped a serious accident!

When he finally arrived at the next station, the conductor asked the agent why he had not telegraphed back that the freight was on its way. The agent said that he had received no message from the conductor.

The next day, the telegraph wires were found broken. Only Dick's message had gotten through.

★ ★ ★ ★ ★

Let's Hear It for Animal Heroes!

Do you know of an animal that has been a hero? Share your tale with other kids at **Almanac4kids.com/TellUs.**

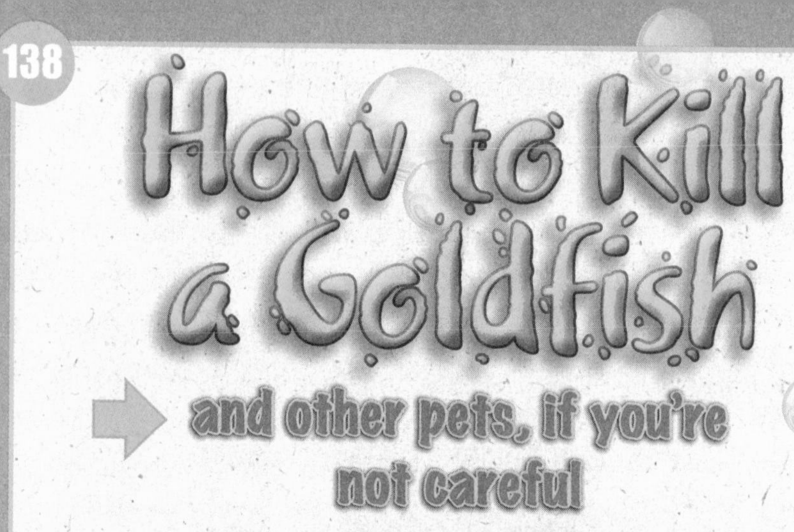

How to Kill a Goldfish

and other pets, if you're not careful

Goldfish

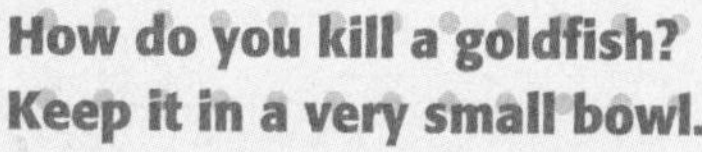

How do you kill a goldfish? Keep it in a very small bowl.

Goldfish need space to flex their fins. Make sure that the tank is the right size for your fish (or fishes). Allow 6 to 8 gallons of water for each adult fish. Change it regularly and use a filtration system. Keep the tank away from cold drafts and direct sunlight.

TURTLE

**How do you kill a turtle?
Keep it in a dry location with very little humidity.**

Turtles need water. If the environment is too dry, your turtle may develop illnesses. Use a spray bottle to mist your turtle daily. Place a shallow dish with water inside the aquarium so that your turtle can take a dip whenever it wants. Make sure that the pool has fresh water daily.

Hamster

**How do you kill a hamster?
Give it a bath every day.**

Never bathe your hamster unless it has a toxic substance–such as paint or varnish–in its fur that will make it sick if it licks it off. Bathing your hamster destroys the natural oils that are present in its fur and protect it from cold.

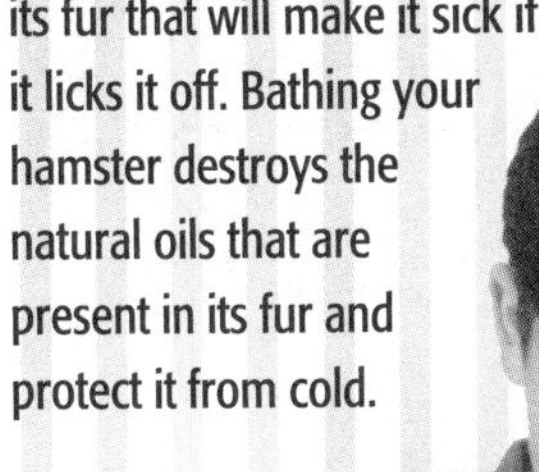

Parakeet

**How do you kill a parakeet?
Give it only seeds to eat.**

For a long and healthy life, your bird needs a combination of different foods in addition to seeds. Feed your parakeet daily with fresh fruit such as apples, grapes, and strawberries and/or fresh vegetables such as broccoli, carrots, green beans, spinach, and sprouted seeds. (Do not feed your bird avocado or chocolate; both are poisonous to parakeets.)

The TRUE STORY of CASEY and the MUDVILLE NINE

Was a school bully really the inspiration for one of baseball's greatest tales?

Ernest Lawrence Thayer was born in Lawrence, Massachusetts, on August 14, 1863. As a boy, he loved sports, especially baseball, but he was frail and avoided rough-and-tumble games. When he was in high school, Ernest earned many scholastic honors and became the editor of the school newspaper. In articles, he often made wisecracks about rowdy students.

One of Ernest's targets was Daniel Casey, who was a foot taller and at least 80 pounds heavier than Ernest and considered by some students to be a bully. Daniel never started a fight with Ernest, but he picked on him and teased him so much that Ernest gave up his wisecracks—but not his love of writing.

In 1886, Ernest moved to San Francisco to write a humor column and ballads (stories in rhyme) for that city's *Examiner* newspaper.

Ernest held that job for 2 years, until ill health forced him to quit. He wrote his last ballad for the *Examiner,* titled "Casey at the Bat: A Ballad of the Republic Sung in the Year 1888," in only 2 hours. It was published on June 3, 1888, and Ernest was paid five dollars for it.

Later that summer, in New York, an actor and sports fan named William DeWolf Hopper needed an idea for a show. When he decided to stage a "baseball night," a friend said, "I've just the thing for you—it's a baseball poem, and it's a humdinger."

Ernest Lawrence Thayer

The poem was "Casey at the Bat." DeWolf, as he was known, recited it from memory and the audience went wild. Soon, newspapers and magazines across the country reprinted it, and people everywhere were retelling the tale of Casey and the Mudville nine. Today, Casey is one of the most famous figures in baseball.

CONTINUED

CASEY AT THE BAT

by Ernest Lawrence Thayer

The outlook wasn't brilliant for the Mudville nine that day;
The score stood four to two with but one inning more to play.
And then when Cooney died at first, and Burrows did the same,
A sickly silence fell upon the patrons of the game.

A straggling few got up to go in deep despair. The rest
Clung to that hope which springs eternal in the human breast.
They thought, "If only Casey could but get a whack at that–
We'd put up even money now with Casey at the bat."

But Flynn preceded Casey, as did also Jimmy Blake,
And the former was a lulu and the latter was a cake;
So upon that stricken multitude grim melancholy sat,
For there seemed but little chance of Casey's getting to the bat.

But Flynn let drive a single, to the wonderment of all,
And Blake, the much despis-ed, tore the cover off the ball;
And when the dust had lifted and the men saw what had occurred,
There was Jimmy safe at second and Flynn a-hugging third.

Then from five thousand throats and more there rose a lusty yell;
It rumbled through the valley, it rattled in the dell;
It knocked upon the mountain and recoiled upon the flat,
For Casey, mighty Casey, was advancing to the bat.

There was ease in Casey's manner as he stepped into his place.
There was pride in Casey's bearing and a smile on Casey's face.
And when, responding to the cheers, he lightly doffed his hat,
No stranger in the crowd could doubt 'twas Casey at the bat.

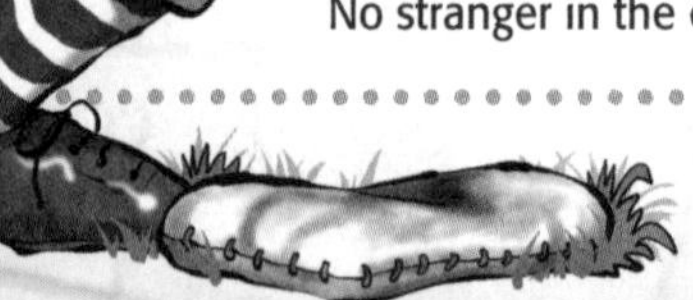

Ten thousand eyes were on him as he rubbed his hands with dirt;
Five thousand tongues applauded when he wiped them on his shirt.
Then while the writhing pitcher ground the ball into his hip,
Defiance gleamed in Casey's eye, a sneer curled Casey's lip.

And now the leather-covered sphere came hurtling through the air,
And Casey stood a-watching it in haughty grandeur there.
Close by the sturdy batsman the ball unheeded sped–
"That ain't my style," said Casey–"Strike one," the umpire said.

From benches, black with people, there went up a muffled roar,
Like the beating of the storm-waves on a stern and distant shore.
"Kill him! Kill the umpire!" shouted someone on the stand;
And it's likely they'd have killed him had not Casey raised his hand.

With a smile of Christian charity, great Casey's visage shone;
He stilled the rising tumult; he bade the game go on;
He signaled to the pitcher, and once more the spheroid flew;
But Casey still ignored it, and the umpire said, "Strike two."

"Fraud!" cried the maddened thousands, and the echo answered, "Fraud!"
But one scornful look from Casey and the audience was awed.
They saw his face grow stern and cold, they saw his muscles strain,
And they knew that Casey wouldn't let that ball go by again.

The sneer is gone from Casey's lip, his teeth are clenched in hate;
He pounds with cruel violence his bat upon the plate.
And now the pitcher holds the ball, and now he lets it go,
And now the air is shattered by the force of Casey's blow.

Oh, somewhere in this favored land the Sun is shining bright;
A band is playing somewhere, and somewhere hearts are light;
And somewhere men are laughing, and somewhere children shout;
But there is no joy in Mudville–mighty Casey has struck out.

–*from* The San Francisco Examiner, *June 3, 1888*

THE PHIN-ISH

Ernest used the pen name "Phin." After "Casey at the Bat" became well known, many others tried to take credit for writing the poem. It was only years later that Ernest revealed himself as the true author.

Backyard DISC GOLF

It's golf with a Frisbee® and a "hole" lot of fun!

In backyard disc golf, you throw a plastic disc to hit targets. You design the course and use any plastic disc that you have.

Each target (and the path to it) is a "hole."

Each throw is a "stroke."

You start from a "tee."

The minimum number of strokes that it should take you to complete a hole is "par."

"Mando" is slang for "mandatory"; it means that you must play the hole as directed.

The player with the lowest total number of strokes is the winner.

For a simple 6-hole course, you will need:

- **1 tall obstacle (a stepladder, ski pole, or badminton net pole)**
- **1 hula hoop or snow saucer, or string (to make a circle)**
- **5 large (3x3-foot or bigger) pieces of cardboard or plywood**
- **4 large containers (baskets, wastebaskets, barrels, or cardboard boxes)**
- **2 chairs**
- **4 towels or blankets**
- **6 stones (for tee markers)**
- **1 plastic throwing disc per player**

On Target . . .

Golf with a flying disc was being played by kids in Vancouver, British Columbia, in the 1920s.

"Steady Ed" Headrick, a Pasadena, California, employee of Wham-O Inc., the manufacturer of Frisbees, coined the term "disc golf."

Today, there is a Disc Golf Association (www.discgolfassoc.com) and more than 3,000 courses in parks or fields around the world.

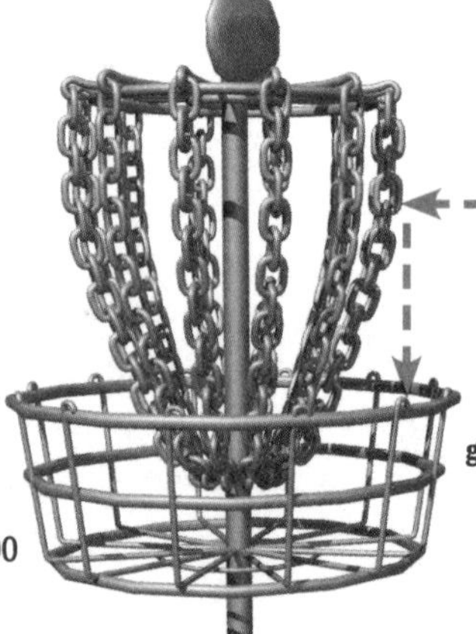

A standard disc golf target. When the disc hits the chains, it drops into the basket, or hole.

A Course of Action

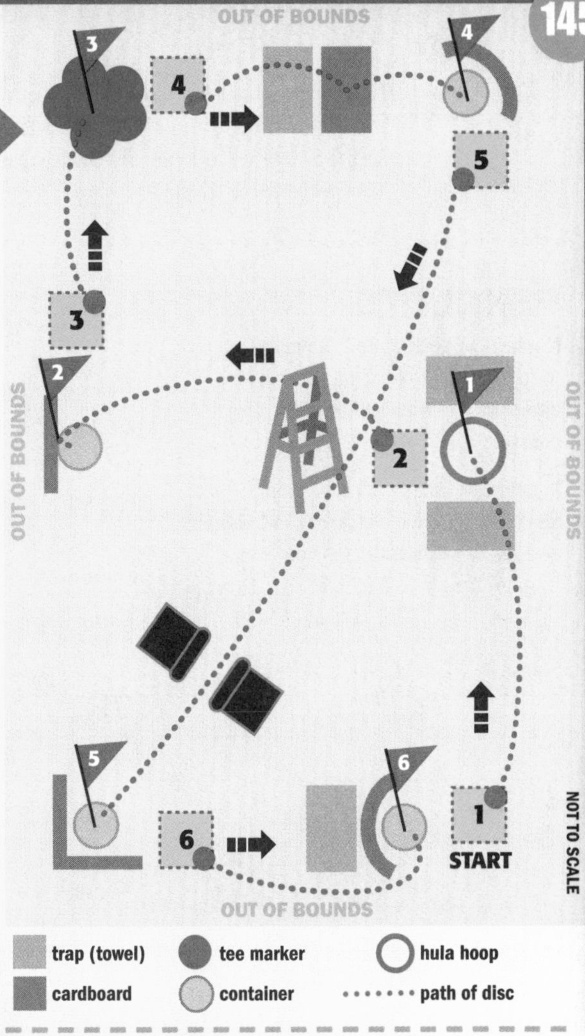

HOLE 1: Par 3. In front of and behind the hole, lay down a towel to serve as a trap (like a sand trap on a golf course).

HOLE 2: Par 3, Mando Right. Discs must travel to the right of the obstacle (stepladder). Draw a circle on a piece of cardboard. Lean the cardboard against a tree, bush, chair, or other prop and place a container in front of it. Hit the circle to complete the hole. If your disc also happens to then drop into the container, subtract 1 stroke from your score.

HOLE 3: Par 2. Discs must hit the trunk of a tree or land in the boughs of a tree.

HOLE 4: Par 4, Mando Skip Board. Position a container with a piece of cardboard behind it to act as a backstop. Between the tee marker and the container, place a piece of cardboard to act as a "skip board." Discs must touch this board on their way to the hole. You can try to land the disc on the board and then go again from beside it, or "skip" your disc across it, as you would a stone on water. Lay down a towel in front of the board to act as a trap.

HOLE 5: Par 3. Mando Left. Mando Between. The disc must travel to the left of the obstacle (stepladder) and then between two chairs before landing in a container with a cardboard backstop.

HOLE 6: Par 2. This hole has a "frontstop" in front of the hole, so the disc must go around and behind it and then into the container hole. Set up a trap in front of the front stop for a more challenging hole.

Instructions continue on next page ➡

How to Play

To start each hole, players take turns throwing their discs from behind the tee marker stone. After "tee-off," the player farthest from the hole always goes first, until everyone has completed the hole.

PENALTIES

If your disc goes out of bounds (o/o/b), add 2 strokes to your score and continue from where it left the course.

If your disc lands on a trap, add 1 stroke to your score, remove the disc, and throw again from near the trap (but not closer to the hole).

Don't Shoot a Snowman!

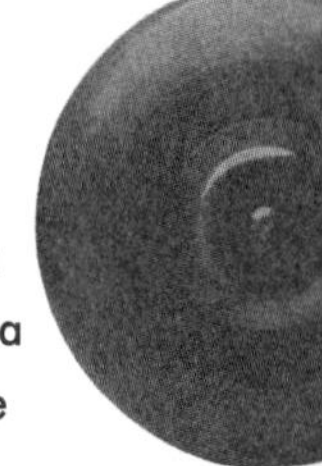

IN GOLF, a high score is bad, not good. That's why in disc golf, players try to avoid a high hole score of 8, also known as a "snowman." (Do you see where the name comes from?)

SAMPLE SCORECARD

								OPPOSITE HANDED							(see below)
HOLE	1	2	3	4	5	6	SUB	1	2	3	4	5	6	SUB	TOTAL
PAR	3	3	2	4	3	2	17	4	4	3	5	4	3	23	40
PLAYERS															

CHALLENGE YOURSELF!

- **Play "opposite handed" and reverse the mandos. Add 1 stroke to par for each hole because you are increasing the degree of difficulty.**
- **Design your own holes and course.**

Tell other kids about your backyard disc golf course at Almanac4kids.com/TellUs.

bluegill

crappie

Goin' Fishin'?

Bring bait that fish will bite.

Freshwater fish love worms! Look for worms in moist areas around springs, ponds, and other bodies of water; in compost heaps; and near tree stumps, rocks, and decayed plants and leaves. If you don't find any, try one of these old-time methods for bringing earthworms out of the ground.

Worm Grunting

After a rain shower, push a 1- to 2-foot-long wooden stake several inches into the soil. Rub a flat stone, steel bar, brick, or piece of wood across the top of the stake. Or, embed two sticks, connect a wire between them, and rub the wire with your stone or other tool. The resulting vibrations are said to imitate those of digging moles, which cause earthworms to flee the safety of their burrows.

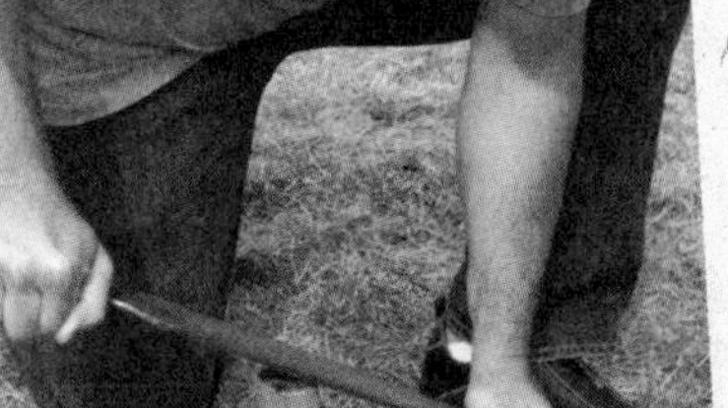

Moles are earthworms' worst enemies; they can eat their own weight in worms in a day!

Worm grunting is also known as worm calling, charming, doodling, and rooping.

continued

Worm Fiddling

Get a 3-foot-long piece of wooden post about 3 inches in diameter. Push it into moist, rich soil to a depth of 3 to 4 inches. Carefully run the teeth of a handsaw back and forth across the top of the post as if playing a fiddle. Some people believe that worms think the resulting vibration is thunder, and they slither to the surface as they would after it rains.

STORE YOUR WORMS

for up to a week in a plastic container with a lid. Punch holes in the lid so that air can get in. Add moist dirt from the same area in which the worms were found, plus a fistful of wet grass. Keep the container in a cool place, such as your basement or refrigerator. Be sure to label the container! If the soil dries out, replace it with moist soil and moisten the grass.

Try these tasty bits on a hook instead:

carrots, potatoes, or parsnips, parboiled (half-cooked) and cut into small pieces

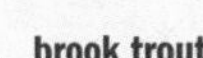

brook trout

fresh or canned corn kernels

brown trout

green peas or lima beans, parboiled

marshmallow pieces

catfish

smallmouth bass

½ cup flour
½ cup cornmeal
pinch of salt

Combine the ingredients in a bowl. Add water, a spoonful at a time, mixing after each, to form a smooth dough. Roll and pat the dough into a ball. Bring a pot of water to boil (ask an adult for help). Drop the dough into the water and cook for 20 minutes. Remove the dough ball from the water, set it aside to cool, and then wrap it in plastic wrap before storing it in the refrigerator. When you go fishing, bring your dough ball. As needed, pinch off bits of dough and form into small balls for your hook.

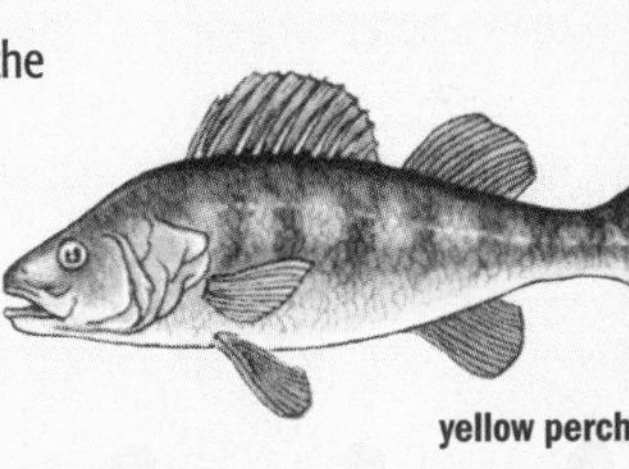

yellow perch

NOTE: Fish are not drawn to scale.

YO! Let's POGO!

In 1919, Gimbel Brothers Department Store in New York City ordered a shipload of wooden pogo sticks from Germany. When the ship docked, the store managers discovered that the sticks had warped and rotted in the humid ocean air. They contacted George Hansburg, a toy designer, to make a pogo stick that would work properly and last. He created an all-metal model with an enclosed spring.

Soon performers were bouncing on the stage. Before long, everyone wanted one—some couples even got married on pogo sticks! For the next 30 years, George developed improved versions.

THINGS TO KNOW *BEFORE YOU POGO*

- **Use a stick suitable for your weight range.**
- **Wear shoes and a (bike) helmet.**
- **Use the stick only on flat, hard surfaces.**
- **Jump up and down, but not too hard—just enough to keep moving.**
- **Don't push the stick away from you or you'll lose your balance.**

EXTREME POGO PEOPLE

ON MAY 25–26, 1990, Gary Stewart of California set the record for consecutive pogo jumps: 177,737 in 20 hours, 20 minutes.

ON JUNE 22, 1997, Ashrita Furman of New York set the record for distance traveled by pogo stick: 23.11 miles around a track.

ON JULY 23, 1999, Ashrita Furman set the record for the fastest time by pogo stick up the 1,899 steps in the CN Tower in Toronto, Ontario: 57 minutes, 51 seconds.

ON SEPTEMBER 13, 2010, Fred Grzybowski of Ohio set the record for the most back flips in a row on a pogo stick: nine.

EVERY YEAR, pogo-ers at the Pogopalooza event perform tricks as well as compete to make the highest jump, most jumps per minute, and fewest jumps per minute.

JUMPING THROUGH TIME

1960s

gas-powered pogo sticks

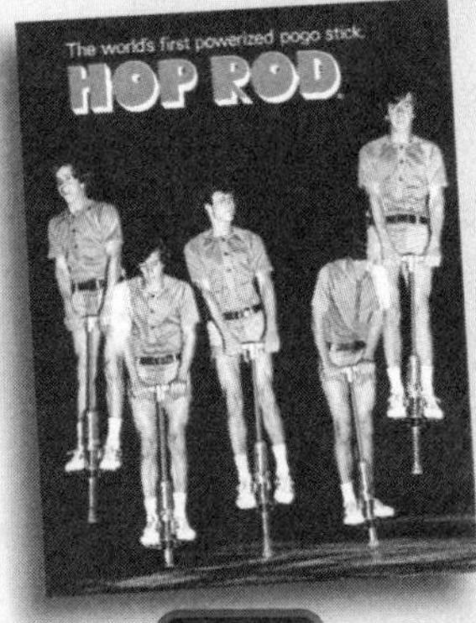

1980s

pogo balls

2001

air-powered pogo sticks

2003

the BowGo, with a flexible fiberglass bow spring instead of a metal spring, enabling jumps of 48 inches or higher

WINNING

Ethelda Bleibtrey grew up with water. Born in 1902, she was raised in Waterford, New York, where from her windows she could see the meeting point of the Hudson and Mohawk rivers.

When Ethelda was 16, she moved away to attend a private high school in Brooklyn, New York. To help in her recovery from a severe curvature of the spine caused by having polio as a child, she joined the Women's Swimming Association and began swimming in a small pool in the basement of a hotel.

Ethelda stands on the block, ready to race.

Ethelda as a teenager (top right) poses with the Women's Swimming Association of New York City.

The Association trainer was a world-class swimmer and water polo player named Louis deBreda Handley. He taught the girls to play water polo, which made them stronger, and introduced them to a stroke that he was developing called the six-beat-double-trudgen crawl (now called the American crawl). Ethelda learned more quickly and swam faster than any of the other girls.

Her first big race was on August 16, 1919, in a pool at Manhattan Beach, New York. Five thousand people had gathered to watch her swim against Fanny Durack of Australia. (Because female athletes were rare, women's sports events drew huge crowds.) Fanny held 11 world records and was considered unbeatable in the quarter-mile swim.

From the start, Ethelda led. To the surprise and joy of onlookers, she stayed in front for the entire race. She won the event, fans' hearts, and a place on the United States Olympic team for the Summer Games in Antwerp, Belgium, in 1920. (She and her teammates became the first American girls to swim in the Olympics.)

Going for the Gold

Ethelda sailed across the Atlantic with more than 200 American athletes. They traveled aboard a steamship that had been stripped of luxuries and used by the military during and after World War I. It was a difficult 2-week trip. The accommodations were cramped and uncomfortable, and the practice pool for swimming in place (while tied to the sides) was 8 feet long, big enough for only one person at a time.

In Antwerp, conditions were not much better. The swimmers slept on cots, eight to a room; had no hot water; and competed in a cold, murky, tidal estuary. Ethelda described the liquid as "mud" but didn't let it slow her down. She set world records in all of her events and won a gold medal in the 100-meter freestyle, the 300-meter freestyle, and a 400-meter relay. One teammate said, "She would have won more, but there were only three races."

(continued)

When Ethelda returned to Waterford, people lined the banks of the Hudson River to watch her swim the American crawl.

A Champion Life

Ethelda's winning ways continued. In 1921, she was the world champion in every event that she entered. In 1922, she retired from competitive amateur swimming without ever having lost a race and having won every national championship that existed, at distances from 50 yards to 1 mile.

She turned professional, taught swimming, and swam exhibitions. She was always proud but not boastful. "Records are like bubbles," she said. "They don't last very long." Later, she became a nurse.

In 1967, she and Coach Handley were inducted into the International Swimming Hall of Fame in Fort Lauderdale, Florida. Ethelda died on May 6, 1978.

The official poster of the 1920 Summer Olympics

FIRST-TIMERS

At the 1920 Summer Olympics, officially the Games of the VII Olympiad, for the first time . . .

- Competitors took the Olympic oath.
- The Olympic flag, with the five colored rings, was raised.
- Doves, a symbol of peace, were released.

Wet Wear

Australian swimmer Annette Kellerman poses in the 1900s in her custom-made swimsuit, designed specifically for serious athletic swimming.

1917

Women who swam competitively wore black bathing suits that covered their bodies from shoulders to toes.

1919

Ethelda and a friend were arrested and jailed because they had removed their bathing suit *stockings* during a workout at Manhattan Beach, New York. (The city council soon changed the law.)

Gertrude Ederle being covered in grease as she prepares to swim the English Channel on August 6, 1926.

1926

Gertrude Ederle wore the first two-piece bathing suit in public during her successful attempt to become the first woman to swim the English Channel.

Fox on the Run

Everyone in Canada knows of Terry Fox. One mountain, 15 roads, 14 schools, a stamp, and a coin are named after him.

Practically from the moment he was born on July 28, 1958, in Winnipeg, Manitoba, Terrance Stanley Fox loved sports. In 8th grade, a gym teacher noticed that Terry and his friend Doug Alward were shy, not-very-tall boys who were crazy about basketball. The teacher suggested that Terry begin cross-country running and, reluctantly, he did. Then the teacher advised Terry to go out for wrestling. This time, Terry didn't listen. He stuck with basketball and practiced hard—but in his first season of organized play, he was on the court only 1 minute.

By 10th grade, Terry was a starting guard. His high school coach, Terri Fleming, admired Terry for never giving up even when a game seemed unwinnable. Over the years, Terry and Doug learned that hard work paid off. As seniors, they were named Athletes of the Year.

Terry enrolled at Simon Fraser University. He began studies to become a high school gym teacher and played on the junior varsity basketball team. Suddenly, at the end of his first year, he had a terrible pain in his knee. Doctors told him that he had bone cancer and that his right leg would need to be amputated 6 inches above the knee. Terry was 18 years old.

The evening before the operation, Coach Fleming showed Terry a magazine article about an amputee who had run the New York City

Marathon. That night, Terry dreamed about running across Canada.

Through 16 months of treatment, Terry never forgot that dream. He joined a wheelchair basketball team. Two years later, he began running with an artificial leg—in the dark at first, so that no one could see him. He trained for 15 months, often with help from Doug, eventually running 3,159 miles and building up enough stamina to run 23 miles a day. His dream was coming to life, with a purpose. He would run to raise money for cancer research. He wanted to raise at least $22 million by asking every Canadian to donate a dollar. Administrators at the Canadian Cancer Society doubted that this would happen.

(continued)

Aching muscles, blisters, and exhaustion filled the days, yet Terry loved his journey. "Some people can't figure out what I'm doing," he said.

On April 12, 1980, with Doug at his side, Terry began his "Marathon of Hope" in St. John's, Newfoundland, by dipping his artificial leg into the Atlantic Ocean. Then, they headed west, with Doug driving a supply van and Terry running 26 miles each day. Their goal was Victoria, British Columbia, where Terry would dip his leg into the Pacific.

On the 15th day, Terry wrote in his journal: "Today we got up at 4:00 A.M. As usual, it was tough. If I died, I would die happy because I was doing what I wanted to do. How many people could say that? I went out and did 15 push-ups in the road and took off. I want to set an example that will never be forgotten."

People along the way cheered him, and many donated money. One day, a businessman named Isadore Sharp pledged $10,000. Another day, Terry collected $20,000 as he ran.

Aching muscles, blisters, and exhaustion filled the days, yet Terry loved his journey. "Some people can't figure out what I'm doing," he said. "It's not a walk-hop, it's not a trot, it's running—or as close as I can get to running. And it's harder than doing it on two legs. It makes me mad when people call this a walk."

By September 1, Terry had covered 3,339 miles and run in snow, wind, and heat on his way westward. He was near Thunder Bay, Ontario, when he began coughing and felt a pain in his chest. When Terry could no longer ignore the pain, Doug drove him to the hospital.

The news was heartbreaking. Terry's cancer had spread to his lungs. Doctors said that he would have to stop running, return home, and start treatment. Terry remained optimistic. "I'd like to see everybody go kind of wild, inspired with the fund-raising," he said.

They did! A Canadian television network organized a telethon that raised more than $10 million. In a few months, donations grew to $23.4 million.

Terry never finished his run. On June 28, 1981, he died. During his life, he had received many awards and been named Canada's Newsmaker of the

Year. Decades later, as he hoped, his example has not been forgotten. Each September, the Terry Fox Foundation holds a National Terry Fox Run Day. There's also a National School Run Day for students, and Terry Fox runs are held in more than 34 countries. Every year, the Foundation raises nearly $20 million for cancer research.

In 2005, on the 25th anniversary of Terry's run, he became the first Canadian-born individual to have his likeness stamped on a commemorative $1 circulation coin.

The Men in Motion

When Terry Fox was recovering from his leg amputation, Rick Hansen invited him to join a wheelchair basketball team. The two young men were about the same age, had much in common, and quickly became good friends.

As a boy, Rick had wanted to compete in the Olympics. However, when he was 15 years old, his spinal cord was damaged in a car crash, leaving him in a wheelchair.

Like Terry, Rick wanted to increase awareness of the needs and potential of people with disabilities. On March 21, 1985, at age 27, Rick began the Man in Motion World Tour. Over 2 years, 2 months, and 2 days, Rick and his team wheeled more than 24,000 miles through 34 countries. He raised $26 million for spinal cord research.

When Rick began his trip, the Fox family gave him a small statue of Terry. Today, Rick continues his mission through the Rick Hansen Foundation, and the figure of Terry sits in Rick's office.

Friends Terry Fox and Rick Hansen in 1979

Rock Paperweights

YOU WILL NEED:

- rounded, smooth rocks
- acrylic paints
- small brush
- clear spray lacquer

1. Wash and dry the rocks.
2. Paint designs or a name on top of the rocks.
3. Allow to dry.
4. Spray with lacquer.

Apple Head

YOU WILL NEED:

- 1 big apple
- paring knife
- 1½ cups lemon juice
- newspaper
- 2 whole cloves
- watercolors
- small brush
- hot glue gun
- yarn

1. Peel the apple.
2. With the knife, carve the nose, make eye sockets, and cut a line for the mouth. (Ask an adult for help, if necessary.) Carve around the mouth to make cheeks, and add some narrow cuts around the eyes and over them to indicate the forehead. For fun, carve the face of a favorite character.
3. To keep the apple from turning brown, soak the head in the lemon juice for about 30 minutes.

4. Remove the head from the juice and place it on newspaper in a warm, dry location for 2 to 3 weeks. (You may notice that it shrinks as it dries.)
5. In 2 to 3 weeks, when the head is almost dry, push the cloves into the eye sockets.
6. Use the watercolors to paint cheeks and a mouth.
7. When the apple is completely dry, glue pieces of yarn to the top of the head for hair. (Ask an adult for help, if necessary.)

Bathtime Puppet

YOU WILL NEED:

felt-tip marker

2 washcloths

scissors

needle

thread

3 buttons, for eyes and nose

rickrack trim to form mouth

yarn

1. With a marker, trace your hand on each of the washcloths (trace a little larger than your hand).
2. Cut out the mitten shapes.
3. Put the hands together and sew around the edges, leaving the wrist area open. Turn the mitt inside out.
4. On one side of the hand, sew on buttons for the eyes and the nose.
5. Sew on a piece of rickrack trim for the mouth.
6. Sew on pieces of yarn for the hair.

CONTINUED

Bread Beads

YOU WILL NEED:

3 slices of white bread
small bowl
3 tablespoons white glue
3 drops lemon juice
food coloring
spoon
plastic wrap
round toothpicks
knife
plate or tray
string or ribbon

1. Remove the crusts from the bread. Tear the bread into small pieces and put them into a small bowl. Eat the crusts or feed them to the birds.
2. Add the glue and lemon juice. Add a few drops of food coloring, if you like.
3. Stir with a spoon until the mixture begins to pull away from the sides of the bowl. Knead it with your hands until it no longer sticks to your fingers. It may take 30 minutes of working and kneading to get the right consistency.
4. Wrap the dough in plastic wrap to keep it from drying out.
5. Pinch off a small piece of dough and roll it between the palms of your hands to form a bead. (You can make any shape you want.)
6. Gently push a toothpick through the bead to make a hole for the string.
7. Continue pinching off dough and making beads. To make several beads all the same size and shape, break off a large piece of dough and roll it into a long rope. With a knife, cut the rope into beads.
8. Set the beads on a plate or tray to dry for 5 days.
9. String the beads to make bracelets, necklaces, or decorations.

Fruity Bird Feeder

YOU WILL NEED:

1 big orange or grapefruit
knife or skewer
string
birdseed

1. Cut the orange or grapefruit in half. (Ask an adult for help, if necessary.)
2. Scoop out the fruit and save it for a snack later.
3. With the knife or skewer, make two small holes on opposite sides of each hollowed-out fruit half, about ½ inch below the edge.

Paper Bead Necklace

YOU WILL NEED:

old magazines or catalogs
scissors
white glue
plastic straws
wax paper
string or elastic thread

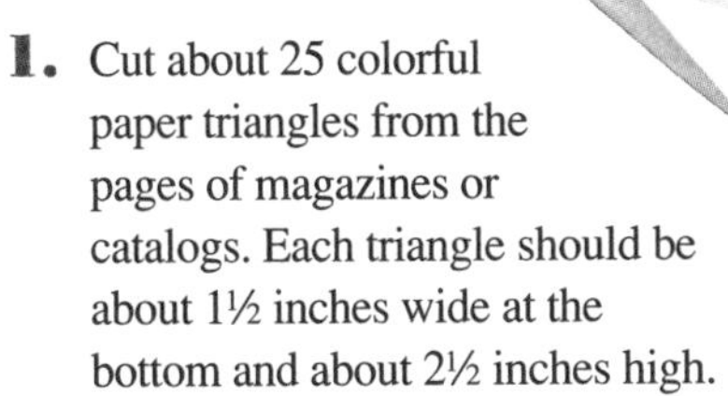

1. Cut about 25 colorful paper triangles from the pages of magazines or catalogs. Each triangle should be about 1½ inches wide at the bottom and about 2½ inches high.
2. Dab glue along one long side of a triangle. Place a straw along the short (bottom) edge of the triangle (the straw will touch a bit of the glued edge). Roll up the paper triangle around the straw.
3. Remove the straw quickly and put the paper bead on wax paper to dry. Repeat for each paper triangle.
4. Set the beads aside to dry for about 4 hours.
5. Trim the ends off the beads to make stringing easier.
6. Cut the string or thread to the desired length. Thread the beads and knot the ends of the string together.

4. Tie a string through the holes for hanging.
5. Fill the fruit hull with birdseed and hang it over a tree branch.

CONTINUED

Handprint Art

YOU WILL NEED:

1 T-shirt or sweatshirt
fabric paints
large, shallow dish
fabric pen

1. Lay the shirt on the grass outside or on some newspapers inside.
2. Pour enough paint into the dish to just cover the bottom.
3. Place your palm in the paint. Remove it and let the excess paint drip off. Press your hand on the shirt.
4. Quickly wash your hands with soap and water. If you wish, make another print with a different color.
5. With the pen, write the date and your name under the print.
6. Let the paint dry and follow the paint bottle instructions to heat-set your design on the shirt. (Ask an adult for help, if necessary.)

Necktie Snake

YOU WILL NEED:

large wooden spoon
clean, old necktie
thin plastic bags (old grocery bags work well)
needle
thread
2 small buttons
red felt
scissors

1. Use the end of the spoon to stuff the necktie with the plastic bags.
2. Sew the open ends of the tie closed.
3. At the wide end of the tie, sew on the buttons for eyes.
4. Cut off a long, narrow strip of felt. Cut a notch in one end of the strip to create a forked tongue.
5. Sew the tongue to the bottom of the wide end of the tie.

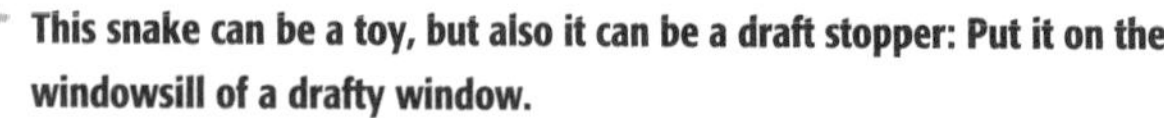

This snake can be a toy, but also it can be a draft stopper: Put it on the windowsill of a drafty window.

Handy Hand

YOU WILL NEED:

1 knit glove
polyester fill
metal canning lid and screw-on band
needle
thread
white glue
lace or ribbon for trim

1. Stuff the glove with the polyester fill until it is almost full.
2. Place the metal canning lid over the stuffing just inside the bottom edges of the glove's wrist.
3. Sew long, crisscrossing stitches over the lid to join the bottom edges of the wrist securely.
4. Dab a bit of glue into the inside of the screw band, then fit it gently onto the canning lid over the glove. (This is the base of the hand.)
5. Glue lace or ribbon around the base to cover the band.

Personalized Wastebasket

Look for buckets at paint stores, craft supply shops, flea markets, or discount and hardware stores.

YOU WILL NEED:

1 tin or galvanized steel bucket
enamel paints
small paintbrushes
buttons
glue

1. Paint the bucket one color and let it dry.
2. Using two different colors, paint stripes around the top.
3. With a bright color, paint flowers around the bucket. Use green paint to paint the leaves and stems.
4. When the paint is dry, glue a button onto the center of each flower.

OTHER DECORATION IDEAS:

- **Paint Xs, Os, or other shapes around the bucket.**
- **Attach stickers to your bucket (be sure the paint is dry).**
- **Dab on paint with a sponge cut into a star or other fun shape.**
- **Paint a design of your own, such as a Sun, a simple landscape, or an unusual free-form design.**

CONTINUED

Potato Print Note Cards

YOU WILL NEED:

1 large, clean potato
paper towels
X-Acto knife or small carving tool
poster or acrylic paints
shallow dish
scrap paper
plain or colored note card paper or construction paper

1. Cut the potato in half. Store one half in a plastic bag.
2. Dry the cut surface of the potato with a paper towel.
3. Use the X-Acto knife or carving tool to cut out around a design on the flat surface. Cut about ¼ inch into the potato, leaving a shape (such as a star, your initials, the Sun, or a heart) as the raised portion of the surface. (Ask an adult for help, if necessary.)
4. With a paper towel, blot any excess moisture off the potato.
5. Pour enough paint into the dish to just cover the bottom.
6. Dip the cut side of the potato into the paint.
7. Press the potato on a piece of scrap paper to see how your design looks before printing it on your cards.
8. Use the other potato half to create a different design.

Try using different designs and colors on the same card. A potato stamp can be kept for several days wrapped in plastic and refrigerated.

Sand Jar

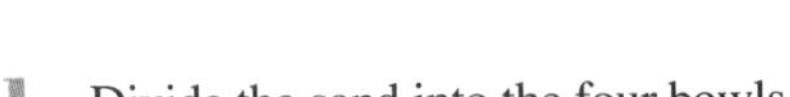

YOU WILL NEED:

white sand

4 bowls

paprika

instant coffee

dry mustard

funnel*

glass jar

straight-sided drinking glass or clean tin can that fits inside the jar and allows about ½-inch space between the jar and the glass or tin can

modeling clay

***You can make a funnel by rolling a piece of paper into a cone. Use tape or glue to keep the paper wrapped.**

1. Divide the sand into the four bowls.
2. Set aside one bowl of white sand. Color each of the three remaining bowls of sand by adding paprika, instant coffee, and dry mustard (one in each bowl), then stirring.
3. Use a funnel, if necessary, to cover the bottom of the glass jar with a layer of white sand. Place the straight-sided glass or tin can inside the jar and stand it in the center, so that its rim is level with that of the jar.
4. Use a funnel, if necessary, to trickle sand, one color at a time, into the gap between the jar and the glass. Make a pattern with the sand and fill the jar to within ¼ inch of the top.
5. Seal the space between the jar and the glass with modeling clay so that the sand won't spill out.

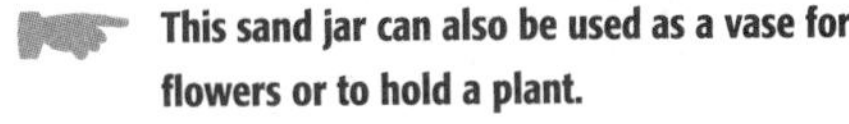

This sand jar can also be used as a vase for flowers or to hold a plant.

STOMACH DIGEST

Through the lips and around the gums,
Look out, stomach, here it comes!

Be kind to your digestive system. In your lifetime, it may handle as much as 50 tons of food to keep you growing and going.

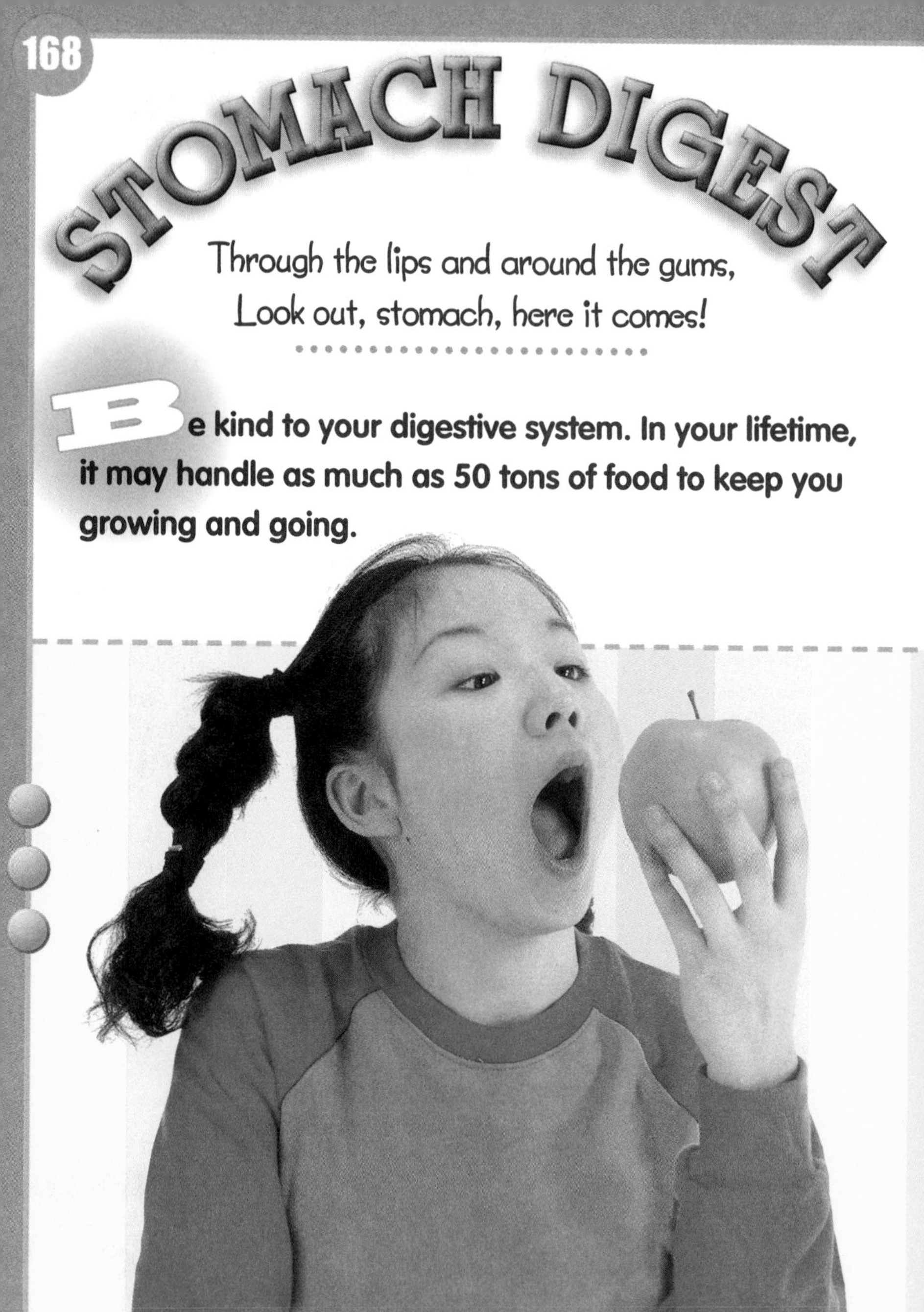

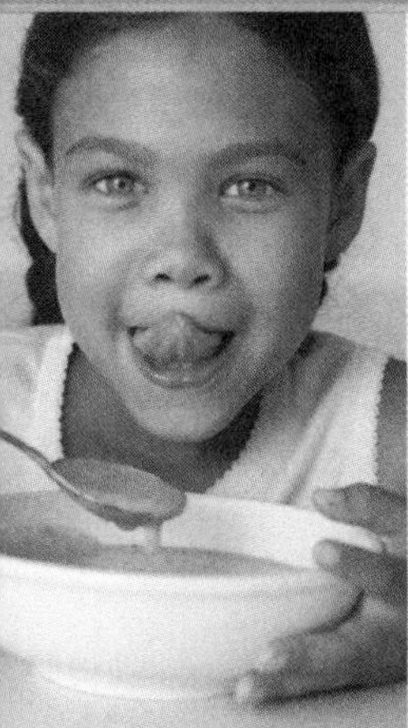

Feeling Hungry?

It's not your stomach "telling" you that. Hunger—and feeling full—is controlled by a part of the brain called the hypothalamus, which also regulates sleep and body temperature. Some scientists refer to the brain's hunger control as the "appestat." Just as the thermostat in your house controls heat, the appestat in your body controls appetite, or hunger. Some researchers think that overweight people overeat because their appestat is set too high.

A Bit About SPIT

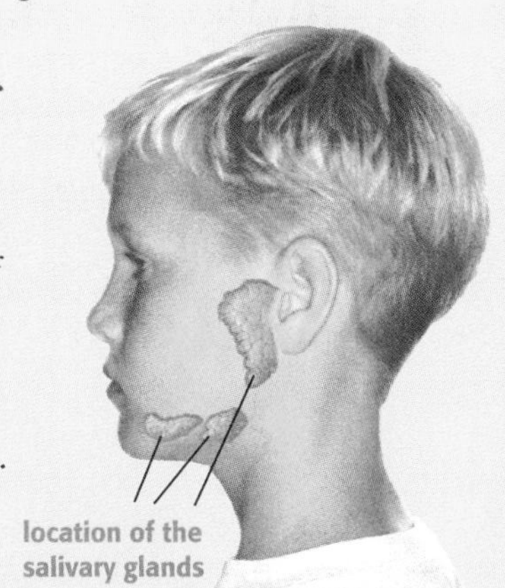

location of the salivary glands

Every day, your mouth produces 2 to 3 pints of saliva (also called spit, spittle, or slobber) to start the digestive process.

Three pairs of salivary glands in the mouth produce saliva, the basic recipe for which is . . .

- **water (about 98 percent)**
- **mucus**
- **enzymes** (such as amylase, which digests starches like rice and potatoes, and lysozyme, which kills germs)

JUICED UP

The stomach produces about 10 cups of gastric juice every day. These juices contain acids and enzymes that break down food into a thick, creamy fluid. (Fortunately, the stomach is coated with a layer of mucus that protects it from its own gastric juices.)

Scientists have demonstrated that gastric juices are strong enough to dissolve some metals.

CONTINUED

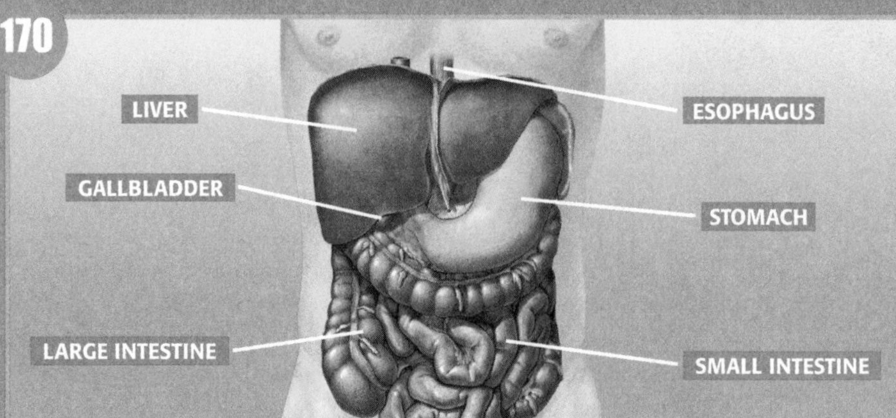

Munch Time . . .

Everything that you eat goes through these stages:

Chewing	**5 to 30 seconds**
Swallowing	**10 seconds**
Stomach digestion	**3 to 4 hours**
Travel through the small intestine	**2 to 3 hours**
Large intestine "processing"	**18 hours to 2 days**

The intestines grow to be up to 25 feet long in adults. The small intestine is not as wide as the large one, but it's longer. It's all folded up inside you; its absorption area is the size of a tennis court!

A FEW WORDS TO DIGEST

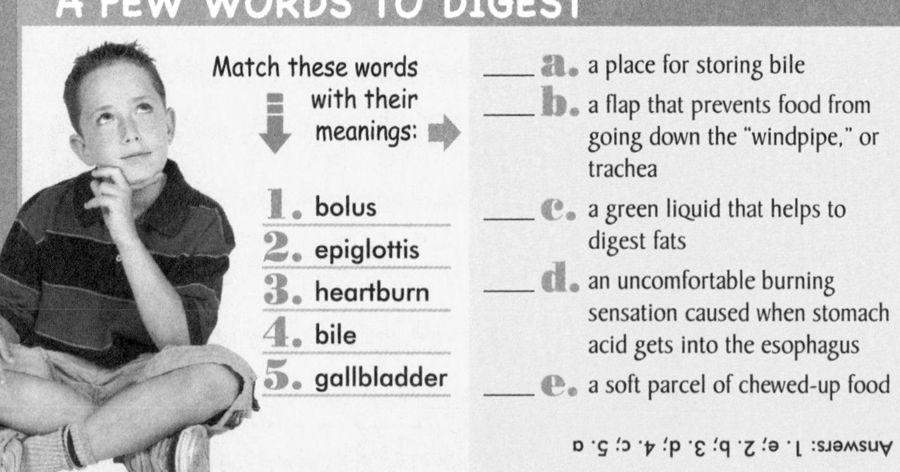

Match these words with their meanings:

1. bolus
2. epiglottis
3. heartburn
4. bile
5. gallbladder

____ a. a place for storing bile

____ b. a flap that prevents food from going down the "windpipe," or trachea

____ c. a green liquid that helps to digest fats

____ d. an uncomfortable burning sensation caused when stomach acid gets into the esophagus

____ e. a soft parcel of chewed-up food

Answers: 1. e; 2. b; 3. d; 4. c; 5. a

DID YOU KNOW?

- The hardest material in the human body is the enamel that coats teeth.
- On an average day, kidneys process about 50 gallons of blood, producing about 2 quarts of urine (as much as what a big soda bottle contains).
- The tongue has about 10,000 tiny taste buds.

Why It's Called "Chewing Gum"

Did your mother ever tell you that if you swallowed chewing gum it would stay in your stomach for 7 years? **NOT TRUE!**

Gum is made from four things, and the body can easily digest the first three: **flavorings, sweeteners,** and **softeners.** The sticky and tricky fourth part is **gum base,** which resists the effects of saliva and stays chewy.

If you swallow gum, your body will digest it, but this doesn't mean that you should swallow it!

HIC-CUP!

Most people have the hiccups at one time or another. Even unborn babies hiccup—scientists believe that hiccupping helps to strengthen their diaphragms.

A hiccup occurs when an irritation to the nerves that control the diaphragm causes it to spasm. This makes you take a short, quick breath, and the epiglottis, a flap that keeps food out of your respiratory system, closes. The sudden closure of the epiglottis causes the "hic" sound of hiccups.

Some causes of hiccups . . .

- **Drinking something very hot or very cold.**
- **Eating too quickly or too much.**
- **Being nervous or excited.**
- **Sneezing, laughing, or coughing.**

- **Average hiccup spell:** a few minutes to a few hours
- **Average hiccup rate:** 4 to 60 times per minute
- **Persistent hiccups:** last longer than 48 hours
- **Intractable hiccups:** last more than a month
- **The most common time to hiccup:** evening

Here are a few ways to stop the hiccups:

- **Pull on your tongue.**
- **Tap or rub the back of your neck.**
- **Hold your breath.**
- **Gently put your fingers in your ears (not too far, though).**
- **Have someone tickle you.**
- **Have someone startle you. (Boo!)**

- **Put your head between your knees and swallow hard.**
- **Place sugar on the back of your tongue and rub it against the roof of your mouth.**

For the Sake of an ACHE

For as long as people have had teeth, they have had TOOTHACHES. Before modern dentistry, some people believed that these old-fashioned folk remedies would make the pain go away:

Get out of bed left foot first.

Eat GRASSHOPPER eggs.

Steal a dishrag and bury it.

Trim your fingernails and toenails on FRIDAYS.

Capture a FROG, spit into its mouth, and set it free.

Pick your teeth with the nail of the middle toe of an owl.

Drive a nail into an oak tree.

Chew the bark of the northern prickly ash tree (known to Native Americans as the toothache tree).

CONTINUED

Some people would rather be ruthless than toothless . . .

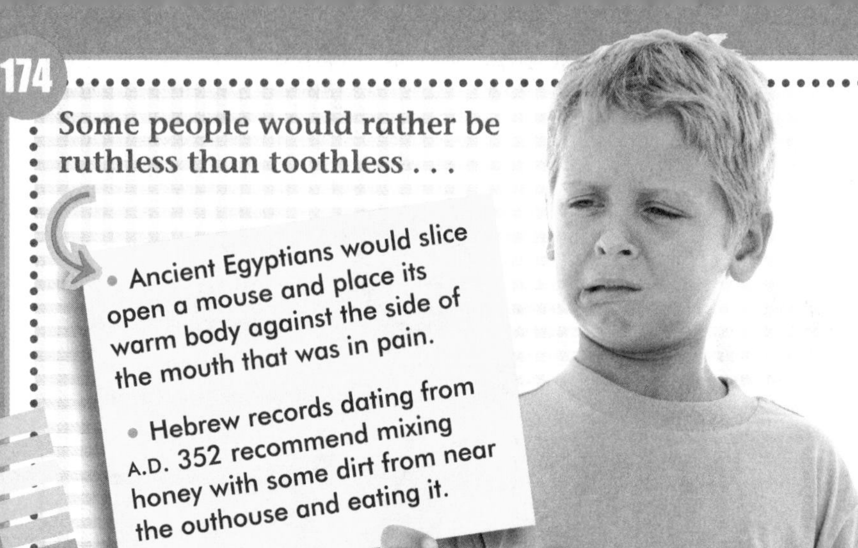

A long time ago, people thought that a toothache was caused by a worm boring into a

Drill Bits

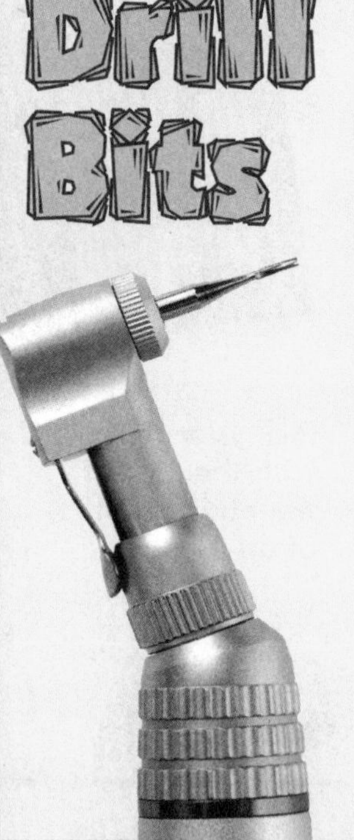

The oldest known dental filling is a bronze wire found in a tooth in the skull of a man who was buried in the Middle East around **200 B.C.** Scientists believe that the wire was an attempt to kill the worm.

In the **2nd century A.D.,** a Roman named Archigenes invented the first dental drill, a thin iron rod with a point on the end. To drive the rod into a patient's tooth, Archigenes rolled it between the palms of his hands.

Gold leaf was first used as a tooth filling in Italy, by Giovanni d'Arcoli, in **1484.**

Laughing gas, or nitrous oxide, was first used as an anesthetic on Horace Wells, a dentist from Hartford, Connecticut, on **December 11, 1844,** while another dentist removed a

Where It Hurts

TOOTH PAIN is often caused by an infection of the tooth pulp (the innermost part, where the nerve endings and blood vessels are) and other tissue underneath the hard enamel. Today, good eating habits, brushing with toothpaste, flossing, and regular visits to the dentist help to keep teeth healthy. If you have a toothache that you can't shake, ask your parents to call a dentist.

Got a surefire toothache remedy? Tell other kids at **Almanac4kids.com/TellUs.**

tooth. In the Orkney Islands, north of Scotland, people still call a toothache "the worm."

perfectly good tooth from Horace's mouth for the experiment.

In the **mid-1800s,** dentists spent 30 minutes, on average, drilling teeth with rods like that of Archigenes, which they rolled between the thumb and forefinger. In 1864, George F. Harrington invented a drill that was wound like a clock and worked for 2 minutes before needing to be wound again. Eleven years later, George F. Green received a patent for the first electric drill.

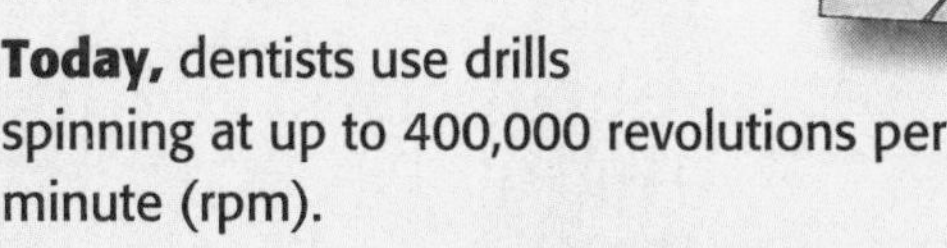

Today, dentists use drills spinning at up to 400,000 revolutions per minute (rpm).

Curious, Amusing, Nifty Anecdotes & Details About CANADA

In June 1685, **paper money** was used for the first time in North America (New France). Because good paper was rare, playing cards were imprinted with various values and redeemed for real money when the next ship from France arrived.

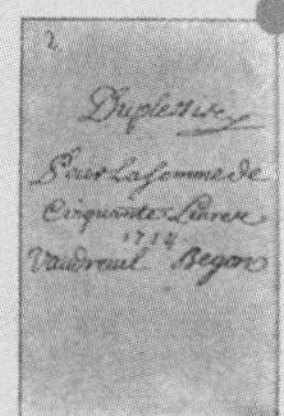

In 1866, workers in Canada's **first cheese factory,** located in Ingersoll, Ontario, produced the **largest cheese ever fashioned by human hands** (the cheese we 3 tons!). James McIntyre, a coffin maker who lived there, wrote a about it titled "Ode on the Mammoth Cheese," making him the country's (and maybe the world's) cheesiest poet.

In 1847, Andrew Downs established the **first zoo in North America** in Halifax, Nova Scotia. In 15 years, it grew from about 5 acres to nearly 100, with parks, a Glass House, and a wide variety of wildlife.

On August 10, 1876, Alexander Graham Bell (who invented the telephone) received the **first long-distance phone call** in Brantford, Ontario, from his father, Melville, who was 8 miles away in Paris, Ontario.

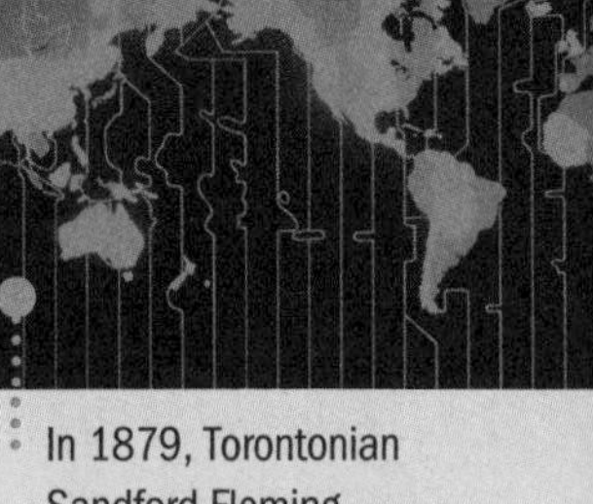

In 1879, Torontonian Sandford Fleming proposed **standard time,** the system for dividing the world into 24 time zones. His idea was adopted 5 years later.

North America's smallest jail is in Rodney, Ontario. Built in 1890, it covers just 270 square feet and still has its original cell doors.

In 1894, Bert Tiedemann became the **first person to bicycle from Calgary to Edmonton.** During the 2-day, 182-mile trip, he suffered a nasty fall when a gopher got tangled in his chain.

On June 14–15, 1919, Capt. John Alcock and Lt. Arthur Whitten-Brown flew from St. John's, Newfoundland, to Clifden, Ireland, making the **first successful nonstop transatlantic airmail delivery.** During the 16-hour flight, the pilots encountered heavy snow, thunderstorms, ice, and high winds. The journey ended with a crash landing.

On April 24, 1895, Nova Scotia–born Joshua Slocum left Boston, Massachusetts, in a 37-foot sloop named *Spray*. When he arrived in Newport, Rhode Island, on June 27, 1898, after having traveled 46,000 miles, he became the **first sailor to have circumnavigated the globe alone.** A few years later, he sailed off once more . . . and was never heard from again.

In 1922, 15-year-old J. Armand Bombardier of Valcourt, Quebec, built his **first snowmobile**—a sleigh rigged up with a Model T Ford engine and attached propeller. He went on to create a business making the snowmobiles we know today.

CONTINUED

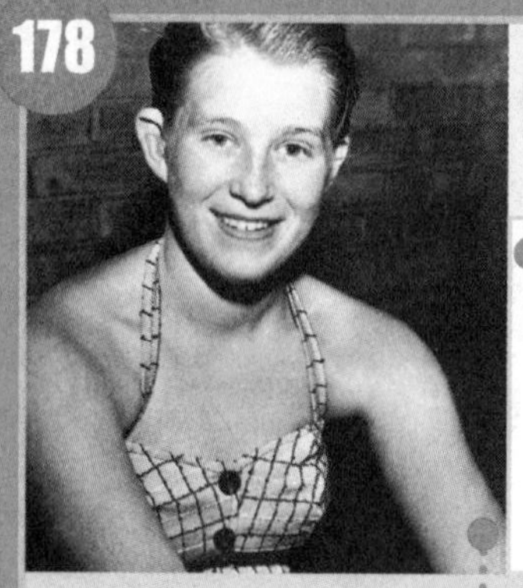

On August 8, 1961, the **world's biggest lake trout** (102 pounds) was netted by Orton Flett in the Saskatchewan end of Lake Athabasca.

On September 9, 1954, 16-year-old Marilyn Bell became the **first person to swim across Lake Ontario.** She swam more than 32 miles in 21 hours, from Youngstown, New York, to her hometown, Toronto.

In 1962, farmer Albert Johnson began clearing his land of rocks and putting them into a pile. He did this for nearly 30 years. Today, the pile, known as the **Great Wall of Saskatchewan,** is about two-thirds of a mile long, 10 feet wide, and 7 to 12 feet high.

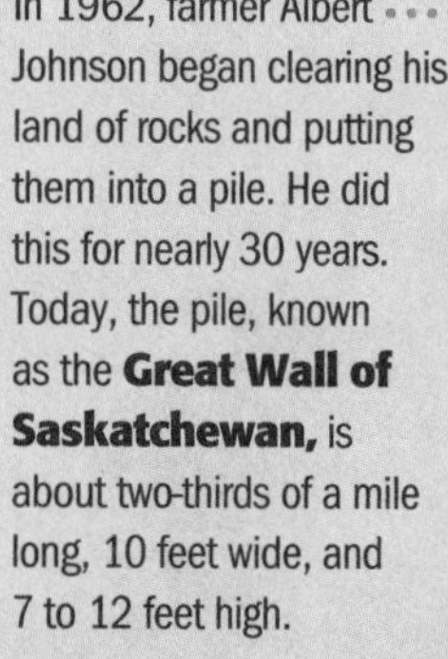

On July 9, 1960, 7-year-old Roger Woodward became the **first person to fall accidentally over the Niagara River's Horseshoe Falls**–and live! He was swept over (he didn't jump) and luckily was thrown clear of the rocks.

In 1986, Sharon Wood, of Halifax, Nova Scotia, became the **first North American woman to climb Mt. Everest.** She and a team of 12 people did it in 2 months.

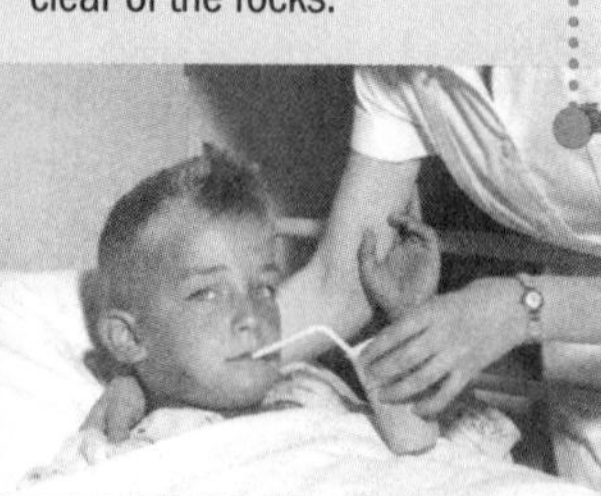

In 2007, the Royal Canadian Mint produced the **world's largest gold coin.** With a diameter of 19.6 inches and weighing 220 pounds, it is worth 1 million dollars.

At the 2010 Olympics in Vancouver, Canada's 14 gold medals set the record for **most gold medals ever won at a Winter Olympics by a single country.**

In Case Anybody Asks . . .

The fastest creature on Earth is the **peregrine falcon.** When diving for prey (small birds, from songbirds to small geese, or bats and other small animals), this raptor can reach a speed of 200 mph.

Reindeer make a clicking sound when they walk. The noise occurs when tendons in their feet slip over the bones. Some people think that the sound helps a herd to stay together in fog or darkness or that when a reindeer walks fast, the clicking helps to warn other reindeer of nearby danger.

The **cheetah** is the world's fastest mammal: It can run at speeds of up to 70 mph. Cheetahs have poor night vision, but their eyes are capable of binocular vision, enabling them to see to a distance of 3 miles. Cheetahs hiss, whine, purr, and growl—but they do not roar.

The only male animals in the world that carry and deliver babies are members of the **Syngnathidae fish family** (sea horses, sea dragons, and pipefishes).

The longest **earthworm** is the South African Giant, which averages 6 feet in length but has been known to grow to 22 feet long. There are about 1,800 species of earthworms.

AMERICA'S Greatest Hoax

In 1866, George Hull, a farmer from Binghamton, New York, visited his sister in Ackley, Iowa. While there, he got into an argument over whether giant people had ever walked the Earth. George believed that they had, but this argument convinced him that there were probably thousands of people who did not believe in giants. George began to think that folks would probably pay money to see a colossal *something* as proof.

So he planned to have one made.

In June 1868, in Fort Dodge, Iowa, George purchased a block of gypsum measuring 12x4x2 feet and had it shipped by rail to the studio of Edward Burkhardt, a stonecutter in Chicago, Illinois. George traveled to Chicago separately. When he arrived at the studio, he instructed

Edward to carve the block in his likeness. Edward took great care to capture the details in George's face, down to skin pores and veins, and he added dingy brown coloring to make the statue look aged. The finished figure measured 10 feet 4½ inches in height and weighed 2,990 pounds.

George then asked a relative, William C. Newell, of Cardiff, New York, to bury the "Giant" behind his barn. William agreed, and the Giant was transported to Cardiff. The burial was completed by lantern light one night in November.

The Cardiff Giant is lifted from its grave in 1869. *Opposite page:* the photograph of the giant that appeared in *Strand Magazine* in 1895.

The grave was left undisturbed for nearly a year.

On October 16, 1869, William hired two workmen to dig a well exactly where the statue lay. As they dug, the workers "discovered" the Giant—as William (and George) knew they would.

As news about the Giant spread, things went pretty much as George expected. In less than a week, hundreds of people came to see it and, altogether, they paid over $3,000 for a look at it.

As time went on, people from all walks of life, including several well-known scientists, were completely fooled into thinking that this statue was a real petrified giant. James Hall, director of the New York State Museum, announced that the Giant was "the most remarkable object yet brought to light in this country."

continued

P. T. Barnum offered to buy the Giant for his circus.

Circus showman P. T. Barnum offered to buy it, but George said, "No, thanks."

George organized a tour for the Giant, taking it to Boston, where it also drew crowds. One man, physician Oliver Wendell Holmes, bored a hole behind its left ear yet never realized that the Giant was a fake.

Finally, in 1870, knowing that the hoax could not go on forever, George revealed his secret and explained how it started.

A Giant Afterlife

The Giant continued to tour the Northeast before going into storage in Fitchburg, Massachusetts.

The Giant's final resting place in Cooperstown, New York.

In 1913, a fellow from Fort Dodge, Iowa, purchased the Giant for $10,000.

In 1935, the Giant appeared on loan at the Iowa State Fair.

In 1948, the New York State Historical Association bought the Giant and put it on display at The Farmer's Museum in Cooperstown, New York, where it was labeled "America's Greatest Hoax." It remains there today.

Why do you think that people believed in the Giant? Share your reasons at **Almanac4kids.com/TellUs.**

Why It's Always Good to Have A FEW Barleycorns

The tradition of a 12-inch foot was brought to England in the 11th century by the Normans, subjects of the Roman Empire who were descended from the Vikings. One foot equals 36 barleycorns (grains of barley) laid end to end.

An INCH was the width of a man's thumb. In 1324, King Edward II of England decreed that the inch was the length of three barleycorns.

A CUBIT was the length of the arm from the elbow to the middle finger's tip.

A YARD, or two cubits, was the reach from King Henry I's nose to his royal thumb.

A FURLONG (220 yards) was the length of a furrow that a team of oxen or horses could plow before resting.

A MILE was 1,000 double steps of a Roman soldier. In 1592, Queen Elizabeth I added 280 feet to the Roman mile's 5,000 feet so that it would equal 8 furlongs.

An ACRE was the amount of land that one man behind an ox could plow in 1 day.

A FATHOM was the span of a person's outstretched arms; 880 fathoms make a mile.

ONE METER equals 39.37 inches—or 118 barleycorns.

Symbolically Stated

Alabama's state nut is the pecan.

Alaska's state fossil is the woolly mammoth.

Arizona's state gemstone is turquoise.

Arkansas's state flower is the apple blossom.

California's state marine mammal is the California gray whale.

Colorado's state insect is the Colorado hairstreak butterfly.

Connecticut's state hero is Nathan Hale.

Delaware's state herb is sweet goldenrod.

The **District of Columbia's** official flower is the 'American Beauty' rose.

Florida's state pie is key lime pie.

Georgia's state prepared food is grits.

Hawaii's state gem is black coral.

Idaho's state fruit is the huckleberry.

Illinois's state snack food is popcorn.

Indiana's state flower is the peony.

Iowa's state rock is the geode.

Kansas's state amphibian is the barred tiger salamander.

Kentucky's state dance is clogging.

Louisiana's state drink is milk.

Maine's state fish is the landlocked salmon.

Maryland's state sport is jousting.

The **Massachusetts** state bean is the baked navy bean.

Michigan's state fossil is the mastodon.

Minnesota's state muffin is the blueberry muffin.

Mississippi's state toy is the teddy bear.

Missouri's state amphibian is the American bullfrog.

Montana's state animal is the grizzly bear.

Nebraska's state soft drink is Kool-Aid.

Nevada's state precious gemstone is the black fire opal.

New Hampshire's state insect is the ladybug.

Each state boasts a number of officially designated "state" things that represent its unique characteristics. Do you know any of your state's symbols?

New Jersey's state shell is the knobbed whelk.

New Mexico's state aircraft is the hot air balloon.

New York's state animal is the beaver.

North Carolina's state dog is the Plott hound.

North Dakota's state fruit is the chokecherry.

Ohio's state beverage is tomato juice.

Oklahoma's state vegetable is the watermelon.

Oregon's state nut is the hazelnut.

Pennsylvania's state dog is the Great Dane.

Rhode Island's state drink is coffee milk.

South Carolina's state snack food is boiled peanuts.

South Dakota's state sport is rodeo.

Tennessee's state wildflower is the passionflower.

Texas's state dish is chili.

Utah's state cooking pot is the Dutch oven.

Vermont's state amphibian is the northern leopard frog.

Virginia's state bat is the Virginia big-eared bat.

Washington's state vegetable is the Walla Walla sweet onion.

West Virginia's state fish is the brook trout.

Wisconsin's state dance is the polka.

Wyoming's state dinosaur is the triceratops.

Bird Words

Many popular sayings involve birds.
Match each phrase to the correct meaning.

1. To cook someone's goose

2. Duck soup

3. To eat crow

4. To eat like a bird

5. To ruffle someone's feathers

6. To rule the roost

7. To be a sitting duck

8. A swan song

9. To spread your wings

10. To watch like a hawk

____ **A** To annoy someone

____ **B** To eat very little

____ **C** To be independent and try new things

____ **D** To be easily fooled or attacked

____ **E** Something that's easy

____ **F** An artist's last work or performance before death or retirement

____ **G** To carefully observe

____ **H** To be boss

____ **I** To admit a mistake

____ **J** To ruin someone's plans or reputation

Answers: 1. J; 2. E; 3. I; 4. B; 5. A; 6. H; 7. D; 8. F; 9. C; 10. G

Wet Your Whistle

Can you whistle? People have been doing it for centuries.

To keep your lips and tongue in shape, practice these exercises:

- Open your mouth. Move the tip of your tongue back and forth, touching each corner of it.

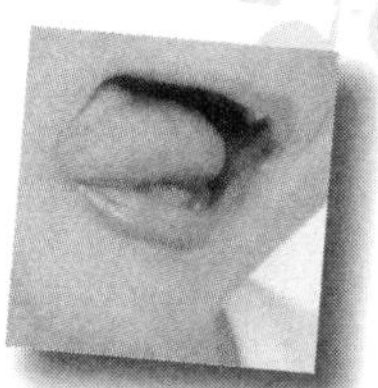

- Stick out your tongue and try to touch the tip of your nose. Relax. Try to touch your tongue to the end of your chin. Relax and repeat both.

- Put your bottom lip over your top lip. Hold it for a few seconds. Reverse and hold for a few seconds.

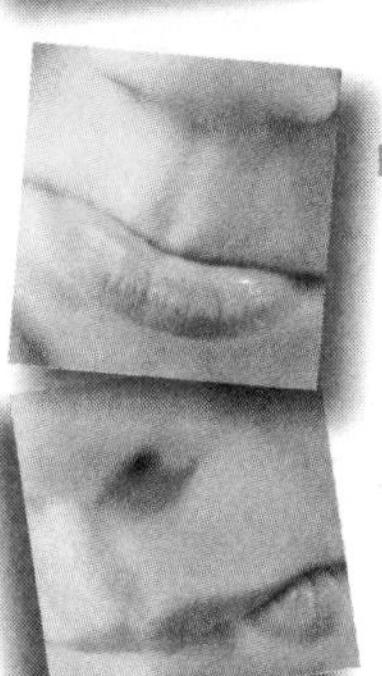

To make the best sound . . .

- Use wax-free lip balm. Wax tends to distort the sound.
- Do not eat dairy products before whistling. Milk, cheese, and yogurt can alter the saliva-mucus balance in your mouth and throat.
- Avoid kissing! It can make your lips mushy.

Now, put your lips together and blow!

People whistle to communicate in China, Guyana, Mexico, Nepal, Papua New Guinea, Senegal, Vietnam, and a few small towns in southern Europe. Students on La Gomera, one of Spain's Canary Islands, learn *silbo* (from the Spanish verb "to whistle"), a nearly extinct whistling language.

ACKNOWLEDGMENTS

PICTURE CREDITS

ABBREVIATIONS:

GCNY—The Granger Collection, New York

GI—Getty Images

NASA—National Aeronautics and Space Administration

NASA/JPL—National Aeronautics and Space Administration/Jet Propulsion Laboratory

The editors acknowledge Thinkstock, a division of Getty Images, as the source for numerous images that appear in this publication.

Front cover: (Boy with glasses) Hola Images/GI. (Boy with globe) Alistair Berg/GI. (Vegetable man) C Squared Studios/GI.

Calendar: 10: (Center left) Abraham S. 11: (Center left) NASA. 12: (Bottom left) NASA/JPL–Caltech. 13: (Center) GCNY. 15: (Center) Lori Adamski Peek/GI. (Bottom) Arbor Day Foundation. 16: (Top and bottom left) Arbor Day Foundation. 17: (Top left) Arborday.org. (Bottom left) Peter Kelley. (Bottom right) Jeff Sullivan. 22: (Top) Lou Eastman. (Bottom) Margo Letourneau. 23: (Top) Margo Letourneau. (Center) Lou Eastman. (Bottom) Margo Letourneau.

Astronomy: 28–29: NASA/JPL–Caltech. 30: (Top) Wally Pacholka/AstroPics.com. (Center) NASA, ESA, CXC, JPL–Caltech, J. Hester and A. Loll (Arizona State University), R. Gehrz (University of Minnesota), and STScl. (Bottom) Jerry Lodriguss/AstroPix LLC. 31: Chris Butler. 32–33: (Top) NASA/JPL–Caltech/ESA/CXC/STScl. (Bottom) Chris Butler. 36: (Top) Marcia Hopper. (Center) GCNY. 37: (Center) NASA, ESA. 40: Photograph by Geoffrey Notkin/Aerolite. Meteorites copyright © Oscar E. Monnig Meteorite Gallery. 41: (Top) Alabama Museum of Natural History. 42: (Top) GCNY. 43: (Top) Mike Copeland/GI. 44–45: Catherine Laplace-Builhe/www.seti-wow.org. 46: (Top) NASA/Kepler mission/Wendy Stenzel. 47: (Top) ESO/Stéphane Guisard. 48: (Top) NAIC–Arecibo Observatory, a facility of the NSF. (Center left) NASA Headquarters–GReatest Images of NASA (NASA–HQ–GRIN). (Bottom) NAAPO. 49: (Top) Seth Shostak/SETI Institute. (Bottom) Harvard University. 51: (Bottom) Margo Letourneau.

Weather: 53: (Top two and bottom two cloud images) University Corporation for Atmospheric Research. 54: (All) University Corporation for Atmospheric Research. 55: (Top) Fraser P via Flickr. (Bottom) Image Source/GI. 58: (Top left) Bethel (Me.) Area Chamber of Commerce. 62: (Top) NASA. (Center) NASA/JPL. 67: (Bottom right) Tammie Dooley/www.soloroadtrip.com. 69: (Top) Ron Hay.

Nature: 70: Steven Puetzer/GI. 71: (Top) Darwin Dale/Photo Researchers, Inc. (Bottom) Brian Brake/Photo Researchers, Inc. 72: (Top) Norbert Wu/Minden Pictures. (Center) Wolcott Henry/National Geographic Image Collection. (Bottom) Paul Zahl/National Geographic Image Collection. 73: (Top) Thomas Marent/GI. (Bottom) Jana Jirak/GI. 74–75: (Illustration) Bob Dacey/Bandelin-Dacey Studios/MB Artists. 74: Tom Chance/GI. 76: (Top left) Carole Nickerson. (Bottom) Retha Scholtz. 77: (Top) D. Keith Meyers. 79: (Bottom) Ian Boddy/SPL/GI. 80: (Illustrations) Kim Kurki. 82: (Left) Gail Shumway/GI. 84: (Bottom) Adam Blanchette, on display at Harvard Museum of Natural History, Cambridge, Massachusetts. 88: (Illustration) Kim Kurki. 89: (Illustration) Kim Kurki. 88: (Bottom left) www.poison-ivy.org. 89: (Top, all) www.poison-ivy.org. 91: (Top) Martin LaBar.

In the Garden: 93: (Bottom) Zia Soleil/GI. 94: (Bottom) Lynne Ronemous. 95: (Top) Rachel Weill/GI. 96: (Right, second from bottom) Fragrant Garden Nursery. 98: (Top) Peter Dazeley/GI. 99: (Center left) VisionsofAmerica/Joe Sohm/GI. 99: (Bottom right) GCNY. 100–101: (Illustration) Nan Brooks/MB Artists. 101: (Bottom) Don Knapp. 102–103: (Illustration) Carolyn Croll/MB Artists. 104: (Center) SOMOS/SuperStock. 105: (Top left) Jupiterimages/GI. 106: (Top left) Alpha Lau/avlxyz. 107: (Top and center) Courtesy of the California Avocado Commission. 108: (Top right) Shari. (Bottom) Michelle Hitchcock. 110: (Top left) Blend Images/Jon Feingersh/GI. 111: (Top left) Anita Gould. (Top right) Andrew Bossi. (Left, second from bottom) Darlyne A. Murawski/GI. (Bottom right) Uwe H. Friese. 113: (Caterpillars 1, 2, & 3) Carla Finley.

On the Farm: 118: (Bottom right) Kurt M. Karlovich. 122: (Bottom left) Scott Indermaur/GI. 126: (Bottom) Aldo P. Biagiotti. 127: (Center right) Sylvia Serrado/GI. 128–129: (All) Aldo P. Biagiotti.

Pets: 131: (Right) GI. 132: (Top) GI. 134–136: (Illustrations) Virginia Allyn/MB Artists. 139: (Bottom left) Paul Bricknell/GI.

Sports: 142: (Illustration) Eldon Doty/MB Artists. 145: (Illustration) Margo Letourneau. 147: (Bottom left) Todd Schmidt. 150: Kate Connell/GI. 151: (Top) Koveleski. (Bottom left) Fred Grzybowski. (Bottom right) Kate Will/www.LikeTotally80s.com. 152: (All) ISHOF, Inc. 154: ISHOF, Inc. 155: (Center) GCNY. 157: Gail Harvey. 159: (Top right) Coin image copyright © 2010 Royal Canadian Mint—All rights reserved/Image de pièce copyright © 2010 Monnaie royale canadienne—Tous droits réservés. (Bottom) Fred Fox/The Terry Fox Foundation.

Crafts: 160–167: (Illustrations) Renée Quintal Daily/MB Artists.

Health: 170: (Top) A.D.A.M. Images. 173: (Bottom center) Richard Murphy.

Amusement: 176: (Top left) GCNY. (Top center) Fred Perry. 177: (Bottom left) GCNY. (Top right) Mike Dellow. (Bottom right) Copyright © J. Albert Bombardier Museum. 178: (Top left) Canada's Sports Hall of Fame/www.sportshall.ca. (Center left) Niagara Falls (Ont.) Public Library. (Bottom left) GraceKelly. (Center middle) Joan Champ. (Bottom right) Ludek Kovar. 182: (Bottom) Amanda Banner. 184: (Bottom left) Manfred Heyde.

CONTRIBUTORS

Bob Berman: Oh, My Heavens!, 28. **Aldo P. Biagiotti:** A Tale of Two Burros, 126. **Jack Burnett:** Backyard Disc Golf, 144. **Alice Cary:** Look Out, BE-LOW-W-W-W for Meteorites, 38; Calling All Aliens, 44; Creatures That Glow, 70; Why (and How) Leaves Change Color, 79; Be a Bird Brainiac!, 82; This Alligator Grows on a Tree, 106; Winning at a Crawl, 152; Fox on the Run, 156; Stomach Digest, 168. **Gregory Danner:** Meet the Thermometer Men, 64. **Mare-Anne Jarvela:** Cuke-in-a-Bottle, 100; Classic Crafts, 160. **Martie Majoros:** Peas, Please, 97; This Is Really Corny, 114; How to Kill a Goldfish, 138. **Sarah Perreault:** Yo! Let's Pogo!, 150. **Sara Schultz:** Symbolically Stated, 184. **Luisa Silveri:** Saint Bernards: The Lovable Lifesavers, 130. **Heidi Stonehill:** Sirius-ly! It's the Dog Star, 35; Rise and Shine, 50; Get to Know a Grasshopper, 74; The Icky Itch Plant, 88; Bring a Butterfly to Life, 113.

Content not cited here is adapted from *The Old Farmer's Almanac* archives or appears in the public domain. Every effort has been made to attribute all material correctly. If any errors have been unwittingly committed, they will be corrected in a future edition.

INDEX